Finger Food

100 tasty recipes
to enjoy with your
favorite cocktails

ACADEMIA
BARILLA

WHITE STAR PUBLISHERS

EDITED BY
ACADEMIA BARILLA

INTRODUCTION
GIANLUIGI ZENTI

TEXT BY
MARIAGRAZIA VILLA

RECIPES BY
CHEF MARIO GRAZIA

PHOTOGRAPHS
ALBERTO ROSSI
CHEF MARIO GRAZIA

ACADEMIA BARILLA EDITORIAL COORDINATION
CHATO MORANDI
ILARIA ROSSI
LEANNE KOSINSKI

GRAPHIC DESIGN
STEFANIA COSTANZO

CONTENTS

ITALY CONTINUES TO SET THE TREND

APERITIF-DINNER COULD EASILY BE ONE OF THOSE FUTURIST WORDS IN FREEDOM THEORISED BY FILIPPO TOMMASO MARINETTI IN 1913. IT IS AN EXUBERANT TERM WHICH INVOKES THE SIGHTS, SOUNDS, TASTE, TOUCH AND SENSE OF SMELL OF AN EVENT BY LYRICALLY JOINING THE WORDS APERITIF AND DINNER.

AS WITH FUTURISM, A GENUINE GROUND-BREAKING ITALIAN ARTISTIC MOVEMENT WHICH ALSO SET TRENDS OUTSIDE ITALY, THE APERITIF-DINNER, A FASHION WHICH BEGAN IN MILAN AT THE START OF THE NEW MILLEN-NIUM, IS STARTING TO ENLIVEN THE EARLY EVENING IN MANY CITIES THROUGHOUT THE WORLD. THOSE IN THE KNOW IN THE UNITED STATES REGULARLY MEET UP FOR AN APERITIF WHICH TURNS INTO DINNER.

IT IS A WINNING IDEA WHICH HAS ALSO TAKEN ROOT OUTSIDE ITALY. A FURTHER DEMONSTRATION THAT ITALY CONTINUES TO SET TRENDS NOT ONLY IN HAUTE COUTURE AND DESIGN BUT ALSO GASTRONOMIC CULTURE. FOR THIS REASON THE ACADEMIA BARILLA, AN INTERNATIONAL BODY DEDICATED TO THE PROMOTION OF ITALIAN CUISINE, HAS SELECTED ONE HUNDRED SAVOURY APPETISER RECIPES WHICH ARE IDEAL FOR THIS NEW AND LIVELY WAY OF HANGING OUT WITH FRIENDS.

THE FORMULA, COMBINING THE TRADITION OF PICKING AT CANAPÉS AND OTHER SNACKS WHILE ENJOYING A NICE GLASS OF WINE OR SOFT DRINK BEFORE DINNER AND THE EVENING MEAL ITSELF, EXPRESSES THE LIFESTYLE OF THE BEL PAESE MORE THAN ANY OTHER REPAST. THE PLEASURE AND MERRIMENT OF AN APERITIF IN GOOD COMPANY AND THE WARMTH AND RELAXATION OF DINNER ARE THE TWO MOMENTS WHICH PERSONIFY MORE THAT ANY OTHER THE CONVIVIALITY, COMMUNION AND PLAYFULNESS OF THE MEDITERRANEAN SPIRIT.

FOR ITALIANS FOOD IS A VITAL FORM OF COMMUNICATION, A TOOL TO CONNECT WITH OTHERS, PASSION AND FLAIR TO MAINTAIN RELATIONSHIPS WITH FAMILY, FRIENDS AND IN THE WORKPLACE. IT IS THE ABILITY TO TELL A STORY TO A WILLING AUDIENCE. SO WHAT COULD BE BETTER THAN NARRATING LOTS OF STORIES ALL AT ONCE, IN A BOOK CONTAINING RECIPES FOR HEARTY AND DELICIOUS APPETISERS, EACH ONE DIFFERENT TO THE NEXT? WHAT COULD BE BETTER THAN INVITING PEOPLE TO YOUR OWN HOME TO SOCIALISE IN AN ENVIRONMENT OF PLEASANT DISCOVERY AND RELAXATION? IS THERE ANYTHING MORE ITALIAN THAN AN APERITIF-DINNER?

GIANLUIGI ZENTI
DIRECTOR OF THE ACADEMIA BARILLA

AN ITALIAN TRADITION

The concept of the aperitif-dinner originated in Milan at the start of the 21st century as a gimmick to shift the meeting time for dinner towards aperitif time earlier in the evening. Yet it is a new name for an old tradition. The ritual of the aperitif – at least broadly speaking i.e. more a complete meal than light snack – was widely practised in ancient Rome and not to be missed. It consisted of a series of dishes that were so creative, opulent and satisfying (Petronius provides us with a good description in his book Satyricon where he recounts the story of a dinner at the house of Trimalchio) as to receive a round of applause from all the guests. If our ancestors had been more sober, a round of these drinks parties, known as a "gustatio", would have constituted an aperitif-dinner.

Over the centuries the custom of beginning the evening meal with food so hearty that dinner could be skipped spread throughout Italy. Above all in Piedmont because it was in Turin in 1786 that the distiller, Antonio Benedetto Carpano first created Vermouth. But also because the evening snack has always existed in this Italian region. It comes from the peasant tradition of eating something between late afternoon and dinner time after a hard day's work in the fields. The food, eaten in the open air usually in the farmyard, consisted of a series of cold dishes such as anchovies with parsley dressing, tomme cheese crackers, pickled trout, cold cuts, fresh vegetable salads and pickles. Everything was accompanied by a slice of homemade bread and washed down with some tasty red wine.

APERITIF-DINNER IS SERVED

What do you serve at an aperitif-dinner? Bruschetta, savoury pastries, tartlets, mini pizzas, flatbreads, croquettes, meatballs, fishcakes, mini frittatas, rolls, pasta salad, small pieces of vegetables or cheese and morsels of meat or fish. Given that guests usually remain standing to be able to converse and help themselves at the same time, portions must be small – one or two mouthfuls at most – , so they can be eaten with the fingers, or at the very least eaten using just a fork, spoon or cocktail stick without the aid of a knife. We should also remember the words of the famous French chef, Auguste Escoffier who said "what appetisers lack in terms of quantity must be compensated by delicacy of flavour and faultless presentation to make them irresistible."

However artistic impression is not enough on its own, the menu must be varied to guarantee surprise and enjoyment. Hot and cold appetisers should be served giving preference to one or the other depending on the time of year. Repetition of taste and colour should be avoided and the food must be presented so that guests are seduced by their eyes and not just the palate.

A theme can be adopted based on the age of the guests, regional cuisine, international cuisine, fine-dining or rustic, the time of the year or the dominant colour of the food being served. The important thing is to avoid mundanity. The great thing about an aperitif-dinner is that those preparing it and the guests are able to enjoy a whole range of gastronomic experiences. And each experience must be delicious, novel and inviting.

TRICKS OF THE TRADE

The watchword for hosting the perfect aperitif-dinner in your own home is very simple: organisation. Every detail, from the menu to the layout of the buffet to the presentation of food and drinks, must be planned and taken care of well in advance.

If the menu is to be tasty, varied and eye-catching then each recipe must be chosen with care to ensure a good overall combination. Remember that, even though this is an aperitif to replace dinner, it is much better to provide a few perfectly prepared dishes rather than lots which will soon be forgotten. Furthermore the food should be prepared well in advance and then heated up at the last minute except for those dishes which must be cooked immediately before being served piping hot.

The buffet table must be strategically positioned between the kitchen and the sitting room so as to be easily accessible by guests and host alike. The layout of the food on the buffet should allow all guests to serve them-selves without having to queue. We're not in the office canteen! A good idea is to use more than one table. If this can't be done the same food should be presented on different serving dishes at both ends of the table together with plates, forks, spoons, glasses and serviettes so that guests can help themselves from both sides at the same time. All serving dishes should be kept topped up and in order on the buffet table. Half-empty ones should be removed.

Shelves or other surfaces should be available so guests can put down their plates and glasses in a comfortable atmosphere. A couple of bins should be located discreetly so guests can dispose of serviettes and cocktail sticks.

ONE HUNDRED APPETISERS FOR GOOD COMPANY

For this book the Academia Barilla, an international body dedicated to the promotion of Italian cuisine, has selected one hundred savoury appetiser recipes. Some belong to the culinary tradition of the Bel Paese such as arancini di riso, olive all'ascolana, focaccia genovese and carpaccio all'albese. Others use some of the finest Italian ingredients available such as Parma ham, speck, mortadella, buffalo mozzarella, fontina, caciocavallo, tomatoes, artichokes and Tropea spring onions. While others still, such as spicy turkey morsels with mango chutney, are inspired by the finest cuisine from around the world.

Every single one is a delicacy in step with the Italian tricolour. Because the cornerstone of Italian gastronomic culture is sharing. More than anything else the most important ingredient for a successful aperitif-dinner, without taking anything away from the food, is conviviality.

MEATY
SNACKS

APPETISERS USING MEAT AND COLD CUTS HAVE LONG BEEN PART OF THE ITALIAN CULINARY TRA-DITION. THE CLASSIC "ANTIPASTO ALL'ITALIANA" – ITALIAN APPETISER – IS A PLATE OF COLD CUTS, WITH EACH REGION HAVING THEIR OWN EXCELLENT SPECIALITIES, SERVED WITH PICKLED VEGETABLES AND SOMETIMES CURLS OF FRESH BUTTER OR FRUIT. THINK OF THE PLEASING CONTRAST BETWEEN SWEET AND SAVOURY PROVIDED BY PARMA HAM AND MELON. ANOTHER CLASSIC ITALIAN MEAT APPETISER IS ASCOLI-STYLE OLIVES CONSISTING OF DEEP-FRIED OLIVES STUFFED WITH A BLEND OF PORK, VEAL AND CHICKEN.

ITALIAN COLD CUTS ARE EXCELLENT EATEN ON THEIR OWN BUT HERE WE'VE TRIED TO BE MORE ADVENTUROUS. MORTADELLA FROM BOLOGNA IS TRANSFORMED INTO A SOFT MOUSSE AS A FILLING FOR PISTACHIO NUT HORNS. BRESAOLA FROM THE VALTELLINA IS COMBINED WITH FRESH GOAT'S CHEESE AND ROCKET TO MAKE LIGHT, TEMPTING PINWHEELS. SPECK FROM THE SOUTH TYROL IS USED TOGETHER WITH TOMATO TO MAKE TASTY MINI QUICHES. A VERITABLE SMORGASBORD OF MEATY ITALIAN TRADITION.

CHICKEN IS A VERY LEAN MEAT AND AS SUCH IS IDEAL FOR APERITIF-DINNER DISHES. NOT FOR NOTHING THE RECIPES USING CHICKEN ARE EXTREMELY VARIED. WHITE MEAT KEBABS, MINI CHICKEN ROULADE WITH PARMA HAM AND VEGETABLES, CHICKEN BREAST IN ALMOND CRUST, CHICKEN WINGS WITH SESAME SEEDS AND CHICKEN AND LEMON CROQUETTES ARE JUST SOME OF THE POULTRY DISHES IN THIS BOOK. TURKEY IS ALSO AN EXCELLENT MEAT TO SERVE WITH DRINKS. HERE WE HAVE INCLUDED A RECIPE FOR DELICIOUS SPICY TURKEY MORSELS WITH MANGO CHUTNEY.

MEAT WHICH IS USUALLY SERVED AS A MAIN COURSE CAN ALSO BE USED AS THE MAIN INGREDI-ENT IN AN APPETISER. DUCK IS A GOOD EXAMPLE. THE RECIPE WE'VE INCLUDED, BITE-SIZE COCOA BREAD ROLLS WITH DUCK BREAST AND CARAMELISED ONION, IS AS TASTY AS IT SOUNDS. LAMB IS THE MAIN INGREDIENT IN THE RECIPES FOR ASIAN MEATBALLS, LAMB CHOPS IN HAZELNUT CRUST AND LAMB KOFTA. RABBIT IS ALSO AN UNUSUAL INGREDIENT FOR AN APPETISER BUT YOU'LL LOVE OUR DELICIOUS RABBIT SALAD PINWHEELS VEAL SALAD WITH VEGETABLES, MUSTARD AND HONEY IS ALSO AN INTRIGUING COMBINATION.

HIGH-QUALITY MEAT CAN ALSO BE EATEN RAW AS IN THE CASE OF FASSONE BEEF TARTARE AND ALBA-STYLE CARPACCIO, BOTH SPECIALITIES OF PIEDMONT. BOTH OF THESE DISHES ARE MADE US-ING BEEF FROM FASSONE CATTLE, A RARE BREED NATIVE TO PIEDMONT. THE MEAT FROM THESE ANIMALS IS SO TENDER IT MELTS IN YOUR MOUTH.

CHICKEN WINGS WITH SESAME SEEDS

Ingredients for 10 chicken wings
Preparation time 2 hours 50 minutes (30 minutes preparation + 2 hours marinating + 20 minutes cooking)

10 chicken wings
3/4 oz. (20 g) mustard
4 tsp. (20 ml) soy sauce
1 oz. (25 g) honey
1 tbsp. (15 g) sesame seeds
salt and pepper

Preparation

Clean the chicken wings to remove any feathers. Break the wings in half and use the part closest to the shoulder. Keep the other half for other recipes.

Bare the bone, season the meat with salt and pepper and marinate in the fridge for at least two hours in a marinade made up of the mustard, honey and soy sauce.

In the meantime lightly toast the sesame seeds on their own in a frying pan.

Remove the chicken wings from the marinade, place them in a lightly greased roasting tin and cook in the oven at 350°F (180°C). After a few minutes pour the marinade over the wings and finish cooking.

Sprinkle with sesame seeds and serve.

SMALL BUT VIRTUOUS

Perhaps the magical phrase "Open sesame!", used in the famous story of "Ali Baba and the Forty Thieves" to open the mouth of a cave where treasure is hidden, actually refers to the magical properties of sesame seeds. They are genuine treasure chests packed full of nutrients able to open the gates of vitality despite their small size. Rich in calcium (800 to 1000 milligrams per 100 grams of product), phosphorous, magnesium, iron, manganese, zinc and selenium, they also contain oleic acid which increases the blood level of HDL cholesterol (good) and lignan which helps to reduce blood pressure. Originally from India where they have always been revered for their multitude of miraculous properties, sesame seeds are probably the oldest condiment known to man. Records of them have even been found on old Sumer clay tablets dated to 2300 BC.

RICE BALLS

Ingredients for 4 people
Preparation time 50 minutes (30 minutes preparation + 20 minutes cooking)

FOR THE RICE BALLS
9 oz. (250 g) rice
4 cups (1 l) vegetable stock
3 1/2 oz. (100 g) Parmigiano Reggiano
cheese, grated
1 oz. (30 g) butter
1 egg
salt

FOR THE BREADCRUMB COATING
2 eggs
1 3/4 oz. (50 g) flour
5 1/2 oz. (150 g) breadcrumbs
3 1/2 oz. (100 g) chopped hazelnuts

vegetable oil
tomato sauce

Preparation

Boil the rice in the vegetable stock until al dente, drain and mix with the egg, butter and grated Parmigiano Reggiano. Check the seasoning and leave to cool.

Mould into small balls, coat in flour, then in the beaten egg and finally the breadcrumbs.

Fry the rice balls in lots of oil.

Serve with tomato sauce.

A THOUSAND AND ONE RICE BALLS

Rice balls, which in this recipe are not stuffed but simply coated in breadcrumbs and fried, are a mainstay of Sicilian cooking. Arancini (from the Italian for small orange) are mini rice timbales which when fried look remarkably like oranges. They are usually served mainly as a mid-morning or afternoon snack, as part of buffet meals and as an accompaniment to an aperitif. They are sold throughout Sicily at specialist fried food shops and come in various shapes and sizes – big or small, round, elongated like a croquette or pear-shaped – and with various fillings including Bolognese meat sauce, ham and mozzarella cheese, ham and peas, ricotta cheese and spinach as well as scamorza cheese and tomato. They are very tasty and, like all fried food, irresistible. Some sources suggest they originated as peasant food, an ideal way for the woman of the house to be creative with leftovers. Others suggest loftier origins as a snack in noble households. Some even suggest the involvement of divine intervention citing nuns in Sicilian convents as the inventors.

FASSONE BEEF TARTARE

Ingredients for 10 small cakes
Preparation time 20 minutes (20 minutes preparation)

10 1/2 oz. (300 g) fassone beef fillet
3 1/2 tbsp. (50 ml) extra-virgin olive oil
3 1/2 oz. (100 g) celery
1 garlic clove
Piedmont hazelnuts
salt and pepper

Preparation

Chop the beef using a knife and place in a bowl. Peel the garlic. Add the whole garlic clove, extra-virgin olive oil, salt and pepper.

Leave to marinate for 5-10 minutes and then remove the garlic clove.

Mould the meat into quenelles or small cakes and garnish with finely chopped celery and whole hazelnuts.

RAW BUT TASTY

Fassone is a rare breed of cattle, native to Piedmont, esteemed since the beginning of the nineteenth century for the quality of milk and beef but also as a working animal. Today Fassone cattle are bred mainly in the provinces of Asti, Cuneo and Turin for the quality of their meat especially the more prestigious cuts. Beef from these cattle is traditionally used in the famous meat dishes from the Langhe including vitello tonnato (veal with tuna sauce), bollito misto (boiled meat) and brasato al Barolo (beef braised in red wine). This exquisite lean beef is also suitable to be eaten raw as an appetiser, like in this steak tartare recipe.

BITE-SIZE COCOA BREAD ROLLS
WITH DUCK BREAST AND CARAMELISED ONION

Ingredients for 20 rolls
Preparation time 1 hour 40-42 minutes
(30 minutes preparation + 1 hour proving + 10-12 minutes cooking)

FOR THE ROLLS
9 oz. (250 g) all-purpose flour
1 tsp. (5 g) unsweetened
cocoa powder
1/2 cup (120 ml) water
1/2 oz. (12 g) yeast
1/4 tsp. malt or sugar
2 1/2 tsp. (12 ml) extra-virgin olive oil
1 tsp. (6 g) salt

FOR THE CARAMELISED ONION
7 oz. (200 g) red onion
1 3/4 oz. (50 g) brown sugar
salt

FOR THE DUCK BREAST
1 duck breast
salt and pepper

mustard
baby salad leaves

Preparation

To prepare the rolls mix all the ingredients together to make a smooth and homogeneous dough. Add the salt towards the end. Cover with a damp dishcloth and leave to prove for 30 minutes in warm place.

Divide the dough into 20 equal-size pieces and mould them into your favourite shapes. Place them in a baking tray and leave to prove for another 30 minutes or at least until they have doubled in size.

Bake in the oven at approximately 425°F (220°C) for approximately 10-12 minutes.

In the meantime peel the onion and slice finely. Place in a pan, add the sugar and a pinch of salt and cook over a low heat for approximately twenty minutes or until the onion starts to caramelise. Leave to cool.

Season the duck breast with salt and pepper and sear in a frying pan, skin-side down first, without adding any other fat.

Place the meat in a roasting tin and cook in the oven for approximately 14-15 minutes until pink.

Cover the duck breast with tin foil and leave to rest for a few minutes before carving.

Cut the rolls in half, spread some mustard on the bottom half, layer a baby salad leaf on top, followed by two slices of duck and a teaspoon of caramelised onion. Place the upper half of the rolls on top and serve.

THE TASTIEST CURRENCY IN HISTORY

Cocoa beans were so valuable to the Aztecs that they became a medium of exchange, the equivalent of a currency. The Aztecs consumed this "food of the gods" in the form of a drink called "xocolatl" which means bitter water. For example a turkey cost 100 beans whereas a small pumpkin was worth only 4.

POLENTA PIECES WITH SAUSAGE AND MUSHROOMS

Ingredients for 6-8 people
Preparation time 1 hour (30 minutes preparation + 30 minutes cooking)

2 cups (500 ml) water
4 1/2 oz. (125 g) maize flour
4 1/4 oz. (120 g) sausage
6-8 mushrooms
6-8 cherry tomatoes
extra-virgin olive oil
salt

Preparation

Prepare the polenta by sprinkling the maize four into boiling salted water. If possible use a copper pan. Cook the polenta for approximately 1/2 hour stirring frequently with a wooden spoon.

Pour the cooked polenta into a greased baking tray to create a thickness of approximately 3/4 of an inch (2 cm). Leave to cool. When cool cut the polenta into shapes using a pastry cutter or simply cut into cubes.

In the meantime wash the mushrooms. Pierce a few holes in the sausage using a cocktail stick and cut the sausage into small pieces.

Place the sausage and mushrooms in a greased roasting tin, season lightly with salt and cook in the oven at 350°F (180°C) for approximately 7-8 minutes.

Remove from the oven. Wash and dry the cherry tomatoes and make a small incision in the skin. Thread the cherry tomatoes, sausage, mushrooms and polenta onto wooden skewers.

Put back in the oven for 3-4 minutes and serve.

A LIGHT FRAGRANT TASTE

The common mushroom, also known as champignon mushroom (scientific name Agaricus bisporus) is an edible mushroom eaten all over the world and appreciated for its gastronomic versatility. Mushrooms make excellent side dishes and sauces. The flesh of these mushrooms is white but turns reddish when exposed to the air. They emit a pleasant odour reminiscent of musk and have a sweet, delicate taste which is stronger in older mushrooms.

SPICY TURKEY MORSELS WITH MANGO CHUTNEY

Ingredients for 6-8 people
Preparation time 25 hours 35 minutes
(45 minutes preparation + 24 hours resting + 50 minutes cooking)

FOR THE TURKEY
10 1/2 oz. (300 g) turkey breast
1 3/4 oz. (10 g) spices
  (black pepper, red pepper,
  cumin, coriander, cinnamon,
  cloves, nutmeg,
  fenugreek and chilli)
1/2 cup (125 ml) plain yogurt
6 1/2 tbsp. (100 ml) coconut milk
1/2 tsp. (1 g) turmeric
1 tsp. (2 g) fresh ginger, grated
salt

FOR THE CHUTNEY
1 ripe mango
3 1/2 tbsp. (50 ml) apple cider vinegar
2 3/4 oz. (80 g) sugar
1 star anise
1 piece cinnamon
1 tsp. (2 g) fresh ginger, grated
1/2 tsp. (1 g) turmeric
2 cardamom pods
1 piece mace
4 red peppercorns
1/2 tsp. (1 g) chilli powder
1/2 tsp. (1 g) cumin
1 tsp. (1 g) coriander

Preparation

To prepare the chutney, peel the mango, cut into pieces and place in a glass or stainless steel bowl with the sugar. Marinate in the fridge for approximately 12 hours.

Toast all the chutney spices (except for the ginger) in a frying pan over a moderate heat to free the aromas and then bash up finely using a pestle and mortar.

The following day pour the mango and liquid into a pan, add the spices and vinegar and cook over a low heat for approximately half an hour, stirring often, until the mixture is quite dense.

To prepare the turkey, toast all the remaining spices (except for the ginger) in a frying pan over a moderate heat to free the aromas and then bash up finely using a pestle and mortar.

Cut the turkey into small pieces (approximately 3/4 of an inch [2 cm]) and place in a glass or stainless steel bowl. Add the spices and yoghurt. Marinate in the fridge for approximately 12 hours.

Heat the oil in a pan, brown the meat, season with salt and cover with water. Simmer for approximately 20 minutes. When cooked combine the sauce with the coconut milk.

Serve the turkey morsels accompanied by the mango chutney.

A SAUCE TO MAKE YOU LICK YOU LIPS

Chutney, the name derives from a Hindi verb meaning "to lick", is the generic name for a whole host of condiments made from vegetables and/or fruits mixed with spices and which originated in India and Southern Asia. Chutney, used as a sauce to accompany meat- rice- and vegetable-based dishes, usually has a sweet and sour taste.

MORTADELLA MOUSSE AND PISTACHIO NUT HORNS

Ingredients for 10 horns
Preparation time 47-48 minutes
(45 minutes preparation + 2-3 minutes cooking)

FOR THE HORNS
10 slices sandwich loaf bread
vegetable oil

FOR THE MOUSSE
8 3/4 oz (250 g) mortadella
2 1/2 oz. (70 g) butter
chopped pistachio nuts
salt and pepper

Preparation

Remove the crust from the slices of sandwich loaf (must be soft and fresh). Pass the slices of bread through a pasta roller to reduce the thickness to one millimeter.

Use a round pastry cutter with a diameter of approximately 3 inches (8 cm) to make a circle and then wrap the circles around special metal Sicilian cannoli tubes. Use water to wet the edges so they stick together.

Fry in oil at 320°F (160°C) for 2-3 minutes until golden.

Leave to cool and then slide the horns off the tubes.

In the meantime prepare the mousse. Dice the mortadella and butter (chilled) and mix using a food processor or blender. Season with salt and pepper.

Use a piping bag to fill the horns with mouse. Dip the ends of the horns in the chopped pistachio nuts.

FRAGRANT MEAT FROM A MORTAR

Mortadella is a cold cut and staple of the Bologna culinary tradition. It is made from pork meat and lard flavoured with spices. These ingredients are cased and then cooked. There are many supposed origins of the name of this cold cut. Perhaps the most likely can be traced back to ancient Roman times. One version suggests mortadella derives from "mortarium" (mortar), the tool used to grind the pork. Other possible origins include "murtatum" which is meat ground in a mortar and "mortarum" which is a pork sausage flavoured with myrtle. In all probability mortadella was first made during the first century AD in an area between the Emilia Romagna and Lazio regions of Italy. The recipe fell into disuse for a long period before coming back into fashion in Bologna during the Middle Ages. Today mortadella is an acknowledged gastronomic speciality protected by the Bologna Mortadella Consortium and European Union Protected Geographical Indication status.

SALAMI BASKETS WITH EXTRA-VIRGIN OLIVE OIL CREAMED RICOTTA CHEESE AND THYME

Ingredients for 12 baskets
Preparation time 30 minutes

12 thin slices of Hungarian-style salami
5 1/2 oz. (150 g) ricotta cheese
2 tbsp. (30 ml) extra-virgin olive oil
pepper or chilli powder
thyme
salt

Preparation

Place the salami slices on small silicone moulds which have been tuned upside down and place in the microwave oven. Turn the microwave on for a few seconds at a time until the salami is slightly desiccated, crispy and has formed into the shape of the moulds.

Use a whisk to cream the ricotta, a pinch of salt, pepper or chilli powder and a dash of olive oil.

Add a few thyme leaves and continue creaming.

Fill the salami baskets with the creamed ricotta cheese and garnish with a sprig of thyme.

A BENEFICIAL HERB

Thyme (scientific name Thymus vulgaris) *is a small bush with green-grey leaves which give off an intense aroma. It is rich in vitamins C and B and mineral salts such as manganese, iron, potassium, calcium and magnesium. Thyme also has medicinal properties and has been used as a balm, an antiseptic, an aid to digestion, an antioxidant, a diuretic, antibiotics, pain-killer and to strengthen the immune system. In cooking it is used as an aromatic herb but also as an ingredient when preserving food and for brine to prevent the formation of mould and to make certain dishes more digestible. If, for example, some thyme is added to the water when cooking pulses or as a condiment for pulses, this marvellous plant can aid digestion and prevent the onset of intestinal swelling.*

CRISPY PARMA HAM POLENTA CHIPS

Ingredients for 4 people
Preparation time 1 hour 45 minutes (45 minutes preparation + 1 hour cooking)

FOR THE POLENTA CHIPS
1 cup (250 ml) water
2 oz. (60 g) maize flour
1 tsp. (5 g) butter
salt

FOR THE FILLING
3 1/2 oz. (100 g) Parma ham

Preparation

Bring the water to the boil, add the salt and the butter. Sprinkle the maize flour into the water. Cook for approximately 1/2 hour stirring frequently with a wooden spoon.

When the polenta is cooked spread a thin layer between two pieces of greaseproof paper or silicone.

Leave to cool and then remove the top piece of greaseproof paper or silicone. Layer the slices of Parma ham on one half of the polenta and fold the other half on top. Use a knife to cut the polenta into the shapes required.

Place in the oven at 250°F (120°C) for at least an hour.

MAIZE THE MONARCH

Maize (scientific name Zea Mays) is one of the world's most important farmed cereals. It is a staple food of North and Central America from where the plant originates. Indeed maize was a staple food in Aztec cooking, just as rice was in Eastern Asia and wheat in Europe. It was usually made into tortillas, tasty, thin, flat pancakes, to accompany numerous dishes based on a wide variety of ingredients including turkey, poultry, iguana, water salamander, prawns, fish, insects and vegetables ranging from tomatoes to gourds. Each dish was seasoned with salt and chilli pepper, both indispensable in Aztec cooking amongst all social classes. Indeed salt and chilli were so important in the Aztec diet that fasting consisted of eating everything in sight except for these two ingredients.

LARGE PASTA SHELLS STUFFED
WITH SMOKED HAM AND RICOTTA CHEESE MOUSSE

Ingredients for 12 shells
Preparation time 30 minutes

12 large pasta shells
1 tbsp. (15 ml) extra-virgin olive oil
7 oz. (200 g) smoked ham
3 1/2 oz. (100 g) ricotta cheese
1 oz. (30 g) chopped pistachio nuts
salt and pepper

Preparation

Cook the pasta shells in boiling salted water and drain one minute earlier than the cooking time specified on the packet. Put them in rows in a baking tin to cool more quickly and coat thoroughly with a dash of olive oil.

Cut the ham into pieces and mince finely using a food processor. Add the ricotta cheese and blend briefly. Season to taste with salt and pepper.

Use a piping bag to stuff the pasta shells. Sprinkle over the chopped pistachio nuts and serve.

AN ITALIAN TRADITION

Ricotta – the name probably derives from the Latin word "recocta" meaning cooked twice – is a dairy product obtained from the coagulation at high temperature (175-195°F [80-90°C]) of buttermilk proteins. Ricotta can be made with cow's milk, sheep's milk, goat's milk or buffalo milk. It can be bought fresh as well as dried or salted, that is to say salt is added for preservation and the cheese is then dried. The latter type is widely made in Sardinia, Sicily, Basilicata, Abruzzo, Puglia, Campania and Calabria where it is popular grated over pasta. Strong ricotta with an intense powerful flavour is a soft, spreadable cheese mainly found in Puglia and Basilicata. It is made from sheep's milk left to acidify in a terracotta container and then packaged in glass jars. Smoked ricotta made in Calabria has an enduring fragrance and a very strong flavour? It is smoked for a few days using chestnut wood and heather, or other aromatic plants, and then cured for approximately one month depending on the type of product required, either a cheese to be eaten on its own or grated.

HAZELNUT CRUSTED LAMB CHOPS

Ingredients for 8 people
Preparation time 26-28 minutes
(20 minutes preparation + 6-8 minutes cooking)

1 rack of lamb (approx. 14 oz. / 400 g)
1 egg
1 oz. (30 g) breadcrumbs
2 oz. (60 g) chopped hazelnuts
3 1/2 tbsp. (50 ml) extra-virgin olive oil
1 3/4 oz. (50 g) butter
all-purpose flour
salt

Preparation

Mix the breadcrumbs with the chopped hazelnuts.

Trim and remove the fat from the rack of lamb (keep the off-cuts for other recipes) to expose completely the rib bones and cut into chops.

Lightly coat in flour, beaten egg and breadcrumb mixture.

Cook in a frying pan with the butter and olive oil over a moderate heat for 6-8 minutes.

FROM MAIN DISHES TO STARTERS

Lamb chops, which in this recipe are tasty, juicy morsels of meat coated in hazelnut-flavoured breadcrumbs, are prepared in a huge variety of ways particularly in Central and Southern Italy. They are widely consumed during the Easter period when they are amongst the tastiest and easiest of festive dishes to prepare. In the Lazio region around Rome lamb chops are marinated in olive oil, garlic and rosemary, seasoned with salt and pepper and cooked on a grill. The best way to eat lamb chops grilled in this simple style is with you fingers. Is there a better way to appreciate the softness and lightness of lamb? Other lamb recipes include coating the chops in breadcrumbs mixed with various herbs and frying or roasting them. They can also be cooked in a frying pan and accompanied with tasty sauces ranging from shallots and balsamic vinegar to mustard and parsley and yoghurt and mint.

PUMPKIN DIP WITH CRISPY BACON

Ingredients for 4-6 people
Preparation time 50 minutes (20 minutes preparation + 30 minutes cooking)

9 oz. (250 g) pumpkin (uncleaned)
7 oz. (200 g) potato
1 oz. (30 g) onion
2 cups (500 ml) water
1 sprig thyme
1 sprig rosemary
1 tsp. (5 ml) extra-virgin olive oil
4 slices bacon
salt and pepper

Preparation

Peel the pumpkin and remove the seeds. Peel the potatoes. Cut the pumpkin and potatoes into chunks.

Slice the onion and sweat in a pan with a dash of olive oil. Add the pumpkin and potatoes and continue cooking. Cover with water, season with salt and bring to the boil.

When the vegetables are soft, blend in a food processor with the liquid in which they were cooked. If necessary dilute with more water and season to taste with salt and pepper.

While the vegetables are cooking, crisp up the slices of bacon in the oven at 250-270°F (120-130°C).

Break up the bacon and serve like tortilla chips with the dip or sprinkle smaller bacon pieces over the top as a garnish before serving.

TASTY AND A SOURCE OF IDIOMS

The pumpkin is popular throughout Italy and has many varied culinary uses. The most famous dish, pumpkin ravioli, originated in the north of the country around Mantua and Ferrara. The pumpkin is also the source of several Italian idioms usually referring to the head. These include "Essere una zucca vuota" – literally to be an empty pumpkin – meaning to be not very bright, "Essere una zucca dura" – literally to be a hard pumpkin – meaning stubborn or pig-headed ("zuccone" or large pumpkin has the same colloquial meaning), "Andare fuori di zucca" – literally to go off your pumpkin – meaning to lose you head or be carried away and "Avere poco sale in zucca" – literally to have a small amount of salt in your pumpkin – meaning a lack of common sense.

CHICKEN AND LEMON CROQUETTES

Ingredients for 15 croquettes
Preparation time 30 minutes (20 minutes preparation + 10 minutes cooking)

10 1/2 oz. (300 g) chicken breast
1 3/4 oz. (50 g) sandwich loaf bread
3 1/2 tbsp. (50 ml) cream
1 lemon
all-purpose flour
extra-virgin olive oil
salt and pepper

Preparation

Remove the crusts from the bread and soak in the cream.

Cut the chicken breast into pieces and blend in a food processor. Wring out the bread and blend with the chicken. Season with salt and pepper. Add the lemon juice.

Mould the mixture into small round balls, coat in flour and sauté in olive oil in a frying pan for approximately 10 minutes. Alternatively drizzle some extra-virgin olive oil over the chicken balls and cook in the oven at 350°F (180°C) for approximately 10 minutes.

KING OF CITRUS FRUITS

Radiant and fragrant. Cool thirst-quenching. Intense and healthy. Lemons (scientific name Citrus medica) *originated in Asia most probably in Southern India, Northern Burma and China. They were introduced into the Mediterranean by the Arabs around 1000 AD. The lemon is the undoubted king of citrus fruits. It is known and appreciated throughout the world for its multitude of uses in the kitchen and numerous medicinal properties. Lemons are a vital component of Ayurvedic and Siddha medicine. The medical virtues of lemons as an antiseptic, in fighting rheumatism and as a toning agent have been known for centuries. They are also an excellent antidote to many poisons. This citrus fruit is even able to produce electricity. When connected to electrodes a lemon is able to power a small digital watch.*

ALMOND CRUSTED CHICKEN BREAST

Ingredients for 4 people
Preparation time 25 minutes (20 minutes preparation + 5 minutes cooking)

7 oz. (200 g) chicken breast
2 eggs
1 3/4 oz. (50 g) flour
5 1/2 oz. (150 g) maize flour
3 1/2 oz. (100 g) unshelled almonds
vegetable oil
salt

Preparation

Remove the skin from the chicken and cut the breast lengthways into strips with a thickness of approximately 1/2 inch (1 cm).

Roughly chop the almonds and mix with the maize flour.

Coat the chicken in flour, beaten egg and then the maize flour and almond mixture.

Fry the chicken in lots of oil, drain on kitchen roll and season with salt.

THE BENEFITS OF AN OIL SEED

Almonds are the edible seeds of the fruit of the almond tree. They are an intrinsic part of the Italian gastronomic tradition, particularly in Sicily and Puglia. Almonds are widely used in the production of savoury dishes and sweet pastries. Some of the many varied uses include almond milk, a tasty, energy-giving drink from Puglia, fragrant and delicious almond granita from Sicily, pasta with almond pesto from Trapani and the chocolate and almond torta caprese from Campania. Moving north almonds are used to make torta sbrisolona, originally from Mantua but now popular throughout Northern Italy, baci di dama biscuits from Tortona in Piedmont, cantucci biscuits originally from Prato in Tuscany and anguilla in crosta di mandorle (eel in an almond crust) from Venice. Almonds are an oily seed rich in protein (24.19 mg per 3 1/3 oz. [100 gr], vitamin E [23.6-26 mg] and magnesium [a cool 270 mg]).

DIFFICULTY

SPAGHETTI FRITTATA
WITH BACON AND PARMIGIANO REGGIANO

Ingredients for 6 people
Preparation time 40 minutes (10 minutes preparation + 30 minutes cooking)

3 1/2 oz. (100 g) spaghetti
1 1/2 oz. (45 g) bacon
4 eggs
3/4 oz. (20 g) Parmigiano Reggiano cheese, grated
2 tsp. (10 ml) extra-virgin olive oil
salt and black pepper

Preparation

Beat the eggs in a bowl with a pinch of salt, the grated Parmigiano Reggiano and some freshly-ground black pepper.

Heat the oil in a frying pan (which you can also put in the oven) over a medium heat. Cut the bacon into strips and cook for a few minutes.

In the meantime cook the pasta in lots of boiling salted water. Drain, pour into the frying pan with the bacon, mix well and add the beaten eggs. Mix thoroughly and cook in the oven at approximately 300°F (150°C) for approximately 20 minutes.

Remove from the oven, cut into small pieces and serve.

THE CHEERFULNESS OF LITTLE STRINGS

It was Neapolitan, Antonio Viviani who coined the term "spaghetti" in 1842 because the pasta reminded him of small bits of string. Originally made in Naples, spaghetti used to be 20 inches (50 cm) long which is quite a long distance to cover with a fork. It was then cut in half, due to restrictions on preservation space, to become the current 10 inches (25 cm). In Italy spaghetti is the most widely eaten and popular of all the long pasta shapes. It is used in traditional recipes and for innovative ones. Spaghetti is ideal for simple sauces such as tomato, olive oil and basil or olive oil and chilli pepper, as well as more complicated ones such as those involving fish Spaghetti is used for many famous dishes such as carbonara and puttanesca and has become a symbol of the convivial and easy-going spirit of the Italian people.

VERMOUTH JELLY

Ingredients for 10 jelly portions
Preparation time 1 hour 10 minutes (10 minutes preparation + 1 hour resting)

2 cups (500 ml) white Vermouth
3 1/2 tbsp. (50 ml) water
6 gelatine leaves
green olives

Preparation

Soak the gelatine leaves in cold water and melt the mixture over a low heat or in the microwave oven. This amount of gelatine will produce a rather firm jelly: Reduce the quantity if you wish to make softer jelly.

Add the Vermouth and then pour this mixture into 10 small glasses. Garnish with the green olives and place in the fridge for at least an hour to set.

You can lower the alcohol content of the jelly by using water instead of some of the Vermouth.

FROM WERMUT TO VERMUT, BY WAY OF VERMOUTH

The standard word is usually the French "Vermouth" but this is actually a classic Italian product. Vermouth (also "Vermut" in Italian) is an aromatised fortified wine first made in Turin in 1786 thanks to the inspiration of Antonio Benedetto Carpano. It was he who Italianised the German word "Wermut" or wormwood in English. It was a way of using young wines with high alcohol content by substituting aromatic herbs for the flavours produced by the ageing process. The resulting product was cheaper then an aged wine but still very tasty. Vermouth, an ingredient in numerous cocktails, is widely used throughout Europe. It is made using sugary white wines with a mild taste and alcohol proof of 95-96 degrees, sugar and a mix of many aromatic herbs including wormwood (scientific name Artemisia absinthium). The alcohol content of Vermouth must be no less than 14.5% and the overall sugar content should be no less than 14 grams per 100 millilitres. The alcohol content of dry Vermouth must be no less than 18% and not exceed 21%. Sugar content must be no greater than 2/5 oz. (12 g) per 3 1/3 fl. oz. (100 millilitres).

VEAL SALAD WITH VEGETABLES, MUSTARD AND HONEY

Ingredients for 4 people
Preparation time 20 minutes (20 minutes preparation)

3 1/2 oz. (100 g) roasted veal
2 3/4 oz. (80 g) carrot
1 3/4 oz. (50 g) peppers
1 3/4 oz. (50 g) celery
2 radishes
1/2 oz. (10 g) rocket
1 3/4 tbsp. (25 ml) extra-virgin olive oil
1 oz. (25 g) mustard
1/2 oz. (15 g) honey
salt

Preparation

Carve the veal into slices and then cut the slices into strips with a thickness of approximately 1/16 inch (2 mm).

Peel the carrots, wash them and cut into julienne. Wash the celery, remove the outer fibres with a potato peeler and cut into julienne. Wash the peppers, remove the seeds and pith and cut into julienne.

Clean and wash the radishes and slice using a mandolin.

Clean, wash and dry the rocket.

Whisk the mustard, honey, extra-virgin olive oil and a pinch of salt in a bowl to make a dressing.

Mix the strips of veal with the vegetables and dressing and serve in small bowls.

SPICY MUSTARD SEEDS

The term mustard refers to some herbaceous species in the Brassicacee and Cruciferae families and the spicy condiment made using the hot seeds from these plants. Mustard was first cultivated in India around 3,000 BC. It was imported into Europe during the ancient Roman period and used as an antioxidant to preserve fruit, vegetables, fruit juice and grape must. It was also used for medicinal purposes to cure rheumatism and muscle pains. Today it is grown in the Mediterranean basin to prepare a variety of condiments used in cooking to enhance the flavour of many meat-based dishes. The most widely grown species are white mustard, black mustard, Chinese mustard and field mustard.

ITALIAN SUSHI

Ingredients for 6 people
Preparation time 48-50 minutes
(30 minutes preparation + 18-20 minutes cooking)

4 1/4 oz. (120 g) Roma rice
2 cups (500 ml) meat stock
1 3/4 oz. (50 g) Parmigiano Reggiano cheese, grated
3/4 oz. (20 g) butter
4 Savoy cabbage leaves
2 3/4 oz. (80 g) sausage
2 1/2 oz. (70 g) ham, cut into small strips
balsamic vinegar
salt

Preparation

Boil the rice in the meat stock until al dente, drain and mix with the butter and grated Parmigiano Reggiano. Leave to cool.

As the rice is cooking, cook the sausage in a frying pan or hot oven for approximately 10 minutes. Remember to pierce the skin of the sausage beforehand.

Blanch the Savoy cabbage leaves for one minute in boiling salted water, drain and place in ice-cold water to cool.

Drain the cabbage leaves, dry using a dishcloth and lay them out on two pieces of cling film.

Spread the rice in a uniform layer over the leaves. Place the sausage on the edge of one of the leaves and the strips of ham on the edge of the other leaf. Roll up the leaves very tightly with the help of the cling film.

Remove the cling film and cut the sushi rolls into wheels with a thickness of approximately 1-1 1/4 inches (2-3 cm) using a very sharp knife.

Serve with the balsamic vinegar on the side as a dip.

FROM JAPAN TO ITALY

Sushi is the Japanese dish par excellence. It is rice served with fish, shellfish, molluscs, seafood, algae, vegetables, fruit or egg accompanied by various condiments including soy sauce, pickled ginger, wasabi and sweet rice wine. The filling can be raw, cooked or marinated and served in various ways including on a bed of rice, rolled in a sheet of dried algae or rolled in rice and then wrapped in tofu which is also known as soy cheese. In this recipe many of the ingredients rolled in the Savoy cabbage leaves are classics of Italian cooking, from Parma ham to Parmigiano Reggiano, and therefore Italian sushi is an extremely apt name.

MINI CANNELLONI
STUFFED WITH FOIE GRAS AND PIEDMONT HAZELNUTS

Ingredients for 4-6 people
Preparation time 22 minutes (10 minutes preparation + 12 minutes cooking)

2 oz. (60 g) rigatoni pasta
4 1/4 oz. (120 g) foie gras mousse
1 3/4 oz. (50 g) Piedmont hazelnuts, toasted
extra-virgin olive oil
salt

Preparation

Cook the rigatoni in boiling salted water and drain while still very al dente. Place in a large cooking tray, to ensure rapid cooling, and mix in with a dash of olive oil to prevent the pasta from sticking.

Coarsely chop the hazelnuts.

When cool, use a piping bag to stuff the pasta with the foie gras mousse and dip the ends in the chopped hazelnuts.

TASTY GROOVES

Rigatoni is a form of short pasta very popular in Italy. It is a tube-shaped pasta with a square-cut end and lengthways ridging on the external surface. It should not be confused with tortiglioni which has spiral ridging. It is originally from Rome and in 1985 was the star of a famous advertising campaign run by pasta-maker Barilla and directed by Federico Fellini: set in a high-class restaurant, an extremely elegant lady is confronted with a menu containing a list of pompous-sounding French dishes rattled off by a flawless waiter. In the end she chooses a plate of… rigatoni. Traditionally associated with sumptuous pasta bakes and rich sauces such as meat ragout, rigatoni is also ideal for lighter sauces such as simple tomato, olive oil and basil or a seasonal vegetable coulis. The stout structure of rigatoni make it able to soak up and enhance most flavours.

MINI CROISSANTS STUFFED WITH PARMA HAM AND CHEESE

Ingredients for 15 mini flat croissants
Preparation time 2 hours 15 minutes
(1 hour preparation + 15 minutes proving + 1 hour cooking)

FOR THE MINI CROISSANTS
4 1/2 oz. (125 g) all-purpose flour
1/4 oz (7 g) yeast
1 tsp. (5 g) sugar
1/2 oz. (10 g) butter
4 1/2 tbsp. (65 ml) milk
2 1/4 oz. (65 g) butter

1 egg
1/2 tsp. (2.5 g) salt

FOR THE FILLING
5 1/2 oz. (150 g) mild provolone cheese
5 1/2 oz. (150 g) Parma ham
valerian

Preparation

Sieve the flour, break up the yeast and begin to mix, adding the sugar and milk.

Finally add the salt and soft butter at room temperature.

When the dough is smooth and pliable, roll into a ball, place in a freezer bag and leave in the fridge for 30 minutes.

Separately mould the butter into a slab with a thickness of approximately 3/4 inch (2 cm) and place in the fridge for the 30 minutes while the dough proofing.

Roll out the pastry with a rolling pin and wrap the slab of butter inside. Now roll out the pastry to a thickness of approximately 3/4 inch (2 cm) and fold in three. Roll the pastry again in the opposite direction to the previous rolling operation and fold in three once more. Wrap the pastry in cling film and place in the fridge for 30 minutes. Fold the pastry in three twice more.

Use a rolling pin to roll the pastry to a thickness of 1/10 inch (3 mm), cut the dough into triangles and roll up each triangle around itself.

Place the rolled up triangles of puff pastry on a baking tray lined with greaseproof paper and leave to prove somewhere warm for approximately one hour.

Brush with egg wash and bake in the oven at 425°F (220°C) for approximately 15 minutes.

Remove the mini croissants from the oven and leave to cool. Wash and dry the valerian. Cut the croissants in half and fill with thinly cut slices of provolone, Parma ham and valerian.

WELCOME TO THE NORTH

Pulled-curd provolone cheese from the Po Valley has Protected Designation Origin status. Provolone originated in Southern Italy and is a variant of provola cheese made in the Campania region. It has been made in the Po Valley areas of Lombardy, Veneto and Emilia Romagna since the end of the nineteenth century.

MINI FLATBREADS WITH PARMA HAM
OR ROCKET AND STRACCHINO CREAM CHEESE

Ingredients for 20 mini flatbreads
Preparation time 1 hour 32-33 minutes
(30 minutes preparation + 1 hour standing + 2-3 minutes cooking)

FOR THE MINI FLATBREADS
4 1/2 oz. (125 g) all-purpose flour
3/4 oz. (20 g) lard
1/2 tsp. (3 g) salt
1 tsp. (6 g) baking powder
4 tbsp. (60 ml) milk

FOR THE FILLING
1 3/4 oz (50 g) Parma ham
3 1/2 oz. (100 g) stracchino cream cheese
1/2 oz. (15 g) rocket

Preparation

For the mini flatbreads, mix all the ingredients together on a pastry board to make a smooth and homogenous dough. Wrap in plastic wrap film and place in the fridge for at least an hour.

Roll out the dough to a thickness of approximately 1/16 inch (2 mm). Use a fork to prick holes in the dough. Cut the dough into small circles using a round pastry cutter with a diameter of approximately 1 1/4 inches (3 cm).

Cook the mini flatbreads for 2-3 minutes in a griddle or non-stick frying pan.

Garnish with Parma ham or stracchino cream cheese and rocket.

FROM STREET FOOD TO GASTRONOMIC SPECIALITY

The piadina flatbread is the most famous culinary export of the Romagna region and has ancient origins. The Etruscans used to prepare a dough using grain flour which was then baked in thin flat discs and eaten as bread or to make sandwiches with a variety of fillings. When the Romans conquered Etruria the piadina arrived in Rome and was soon widely appreciated with a variety of fillings by the well-to-do classes. Over the centuries the piadina became simple peasant food: a flatbread cooked over a hot stone or earthenware and served with a topping of lard. It was during the 1940s and 1950s that the piadina became fashionable and widely popular. It became street food sold from kiosks to tourists visiting the seaside resorts of the Northern Adriatic sea. A fragrant temptation difficult to resist.

MINI QUICHES WITH BACON AND LEEK

Ingredients for 12 mini quiches
Preparation time 2 hours 20 minutes
(1 hour preparation + 1 hour resting + 20 minutes cooking)

FOR THE QUICHES
3 1/2 oz. (100 g) all-purpose flour
1 3/4 oz. (50 g) butter
1 tbsp. (12-15 ml) water
1/2 tsp. (2 g) salt

FOR THE FILLING
1 1/2 oz. (40 g) bacon
1 oz. (25 g) butter
1 leek
1 oz. (30 g) gruyere
6 3/4 tbsp. (100 ml) cream
1 egg yolk
salt and pepper

Preparation

For the short crust pastry cut the butter into small pieces and mix with the flour to form a "sandy" heterogeneous dough.

Add the salt and cold water and mix to obtain a uniform dough without over-kneading.

Wrap the dough in plastic wrap and leave to stand in the fridge for at least an hour.

In the meantime wash and finely slice the leek. Sweat with the butter in a frying pan over a low heat for approximately 10 minutes. Season with a pinch of salt and pepper. Leave to cool.

Dice the gruyere and bacon.

Roll out the short crust pastry to a thickness of 1/16 inch (1.5 mm) and line small individual moulds with the dough. Use a fork to prick holes on the bottom of the dough and fill with the leeks, cheese and bacon.

In a bowl whisk the cream with the egg yolk and a pinch of salt and pepper. Pour the mixture into the moulds and bake in the oven at 350°F (180°C) for approximately 12-15 minutes.

THE ONE WITHOUT HOLES

Gruyere is a Swiss cheese originating in the Gruyères district of the Canton of Fribourg. The product is mentioned in historical records from the seventeenth century. It is made with raw cow's milk which is cooked and pressed. A whole gruyere is round and weighs approximately 77 lb (35 kg). The rind is brown and grainy and the cheese itself is yellow without any holes. Whole French gruyere cheeses are bigger and have holes. Swiss gruyere is often confused with Emmental, another Swiss cheese which has fairly large holes. These holes are caused by the formation of pockets of carbon dioxide during the ageing process due to the propionic acid produced.

MINI CHICKEN ROULADE
WITH PARMA HAM AND VEGETABLES

Ingredients for 4 people
Preparation time 55 minutes (40 minutes preparation + 15 minutes cooking)

12 1/2 oz. (350 g) chicken breast
8 tsp. (40 ml) cream
1 oz. (30 g) carrot
1 oz. (30 g) asparagus
3/4 oz. (20 g) green beans
3/4 oz (20 g) Parma ham
4 tsp. (20 ml) extra-virgin olive oil
1 egg white
mixed baby salad leaves
salt and pepper

Preparation

Clean and wash the vegetables. Cut the carrot into julienne pieces and blanch all the vegetables (except for the salad) separately in boiling salted water for a couple of minutes. Cool in ice-cold water, drain and dry on a dishcloth.

Clean, trim and butterfly the chicken breast.

The off-cuts should amount to approximately 6 1/3 oz (180 g) of meat. Blend this meat in a food processor with the egg white and cream which should be straight from the fridge. Season with salt and pepper.

Layer the sliced Parma ham on the chicken breast, spread the filling over the ham and then place the vegetables on top. Roll up the chicken breast and secure with kitchen string.

Heat the oil in a roasting tin, lightly season the roulade with salt and pepper and brown for approximately 5 minutes. Cook in the oven at 350°F (180°C) for approximately ten minutes.

Leave to cool, remove the string and slice the roulade.

Serve together with the baby salad leaves.

A PULSE THAT LOOKS LIKE A VEGETABLE

Green beans have many different names in Italy including fagiolini: cornetti, tegoline, fagioli mangiatutto. Even though green beans are a pulse just like beans, peas, broad beans, chick-peas and lentils, they look like a vegetable and are treated as such. This is because not only are the seeds eaten but the pods too. They have low protein, fat and carbohydrate content and are therefore low in calories (only 18 kilocalories per 3 1/2 oz. [100 gr]).

HAM MOUSSE LOLLIPOPS

Ingredients for 8 lollipops
Preparation time 3 hours 25 minutes
(25 minutes preparation + 2 hours freezing + 1 hour setting)

8 oz. (230 g) ham
3 oz. (90 g) butter
3/4 cup (165 ml) cream
2 gelatine leaves
chopped pistachio nuts, hazelnuts and almonds
nutmeg
salt and pepper

Preparation

For the mouse, dice the ham and butter (chilled) and mix in a food processor. Season with salt and pepper.

Use a piping bag to fill the silicone iced lollipop moulds with the mouse. Insert the lolly sticks and level off the mousse using a pallet knife or spatula.

Place in the freezer for a couple of hours before removing the lollipops from the moulds.

Soak the gelatine leaves in cold water and then wring them out. Add the gelatine to the cream and season with nutmeg, salt and pepper. Heat the mixture.

Leave to cool. Insert the sticks one by one and then dip them in the chopped nuts.

Place the ham mousse lollipops in the fridge to set for at least an hour before serving.

ON THE TABLE... AND ON CANVAS

Ham is preserved meat. More precisely it is a steamed cold cut rather than one with a casing. It is made from pork leg which is butchered, degreased, boned, left to go high, salted, rubbed and processed and has its origins in the ancient world. Some sources suggest the ancient Romans used to cook huge hind-leg pork joints in water and aromatic herbs. More specifically this dish was prevalent in an area now making up Friuli Venezia Giulia, Lombardy, Piedmont, Liguria and Emilia Romagna. Over the centuries the goodness of ham, a food often found on the tables of nobles, has never been in question. So much so that in 1880 the painter Edouard Manet used a whole ham as the subject for a still life painting.

ASCOLI-STYLE STUFFED OLIVES

Ingredients for 20 olives
Preparation time 1 hour 3-4 minutes (1 hour preparation + 3-4 minutes cooking)

20 large green olives
1 3/4 oz. (50 g) pork
1 3/4 oz. (50 g) veal
1 3/4 oz. (50 g) chicken breast
1 chicken liver
4 tsp. (20 ml) extra-virgin olive oil
3 1/2 tbsp. (50 ml) white wine
1 oz. (25 g) Parmigiano Reggiano
  cheese, grated

1 3/4 oz. (50 g) flour
1 egg yolk
2 eggs
3 1/2 oz. (100 g) breadcrumbs
nutmeg
cinnamon
salt and pepper
vegetable oil

Preparation

Pit the olives by making a spiral incision using a knife around the entire pit.

Keep the pitted olives in water.

Prepare the filling by browning the diced meat and chicken liver with the extra-virgin olive oil. Season with salt and pepper. Add the white wine and continue cooking over a moderate heat for approximately ten minutes. Add a few drops of water if the mixture dries out too much.

When cooked, leave to cool and finely chop. Season with pepper and a pinch of cinnamon and nutmeg.

Add the egg yolk, Parmigiano Reggiano and mix well.

Stuff the olives by remoulding them into their original shape then coat them in the flour, beaten eggs and breadcrumbs.

Fry immediately before serving in lots of very hot oil for a few minutes and drain on kitchen roll.

THE TASTIEST OLIVES

Ascoli-style stuffed olives are one of the most famous foods from the capital of the Marche region and are popular throughout Italy. Stuffing large, fleshy green olives preserved in brine with a soft meat-based filling is thought to have started in the nineteenth century in aristocratic homes. Here was a way of using all the different types of meat available to cooks and the large green olives which had been acknowledged since ancient Roman times for their goodness. Gioacchino Rossini, composer and gourmet, was particularly fond of these olives whether stuffed or au naturel. They were also very popular with another composer, Giacomo Puccini, and one of modern Italy's most famous founding fathers, Giuseppe Garibaldi.

MINI QUICHES WITH SPECK AND TOMATO

Ingredients for 12 quiches
Preparation time 2 hours 20 minutes
(1 hour preparation + 1 hour resting + 20 minutes cooking)

FOR THE QUICHES
3 1/2 oz. (100 g) all-purpose flour
1 3/4 oz. (50 g) butter
1 tbsp. (12-15 ml) water
1/2 tsp. (2 g) salt

FOR THE FILLING
1 3/4 oz. (50 g) speck

3 cherry tomatoes
1 3/4 oz. (50 g) fontina
   (or similar semi-hard cheese)
6 3/4 tbsp. (100 ml) cream
1 egg yolk
nutmeg
salt and pepper

Preparation

For the short crust pastry cut the butter into small pieces and mix with the flour to form a "sandy" heterogeneous dough.

Add the salt and cold water and mix to obtain a uniform dough without over-kneading.

Wrap the dough in cling film and leave to stand in the fridge for at least an hour.

In the meantime cut the fontina cheese into small cubes and the speck into small strips.

Roll out the short crust pastry to a thickness of 1/16 inch (1.5 mm) and line small individual moulds with the dough. Use a fork to prick holes on the bottom of the dough and fill with one quarter of a cherry tomato, a piece of cheese and a few strips of speck.

In a bowl whisk the cream with the egg yolk, a pinch of salt, pepper and nutmeg. Pour the mixture into the moulds and bake in the oven at 350°F (180°C) for approximately 15 minutes.

A FILLING SNACK

Speck is a cold cut from the South Tyrol region. It is made from the hind-leg of pigs which are boned, salted, lightly smoked and cured. The golden rule for perfect speck is "little salt, little smoke and lots of fresh air". Speck, served with homemade black bread and wine or beer, is the classic snack in this Northern Italian region and is often given to guests as a sign of hospitality. The earliest written record of speck, even though it was known by different names, can be found in the butchers' working code and accounting records of noblemen in the South Tyrol from the thirteenth century. Already back then the method used to prepare this cold cut combined two different preservation processes: curing, widely practised in the Mediterranean, and smoking which is more prevalent in Northern Europe.

ALBA-STYLE CARPACCIO

Ingredients for 4-6 people
Preparation time 10 minutes

4 1/4 oz. (120 g) fassone beef ham
3/4 oz. (20 g) mushrooms
3/4 oz. (20 g) Parmigiano Reggiano cheese
1 1/2 oz. (40 g) mixed baby salad leaves
2 tbsp. (30 ml) extra-virgin olive oil
1/2 lemon
salt and pepper

Preparation

Make a dressing using the lemon juice, extra-virgin olive oil, salt and pepper.

Wash the baby salad leaves and put them on the plates. Slice the beef very thinly using a meat slicer. You can harden the meat in the freezer beforehand to facilitate slicing. Season with a pinch of salt and pepper and layer the beef on the salad.

Use a mandolin to make shavings of Parmigiano Reggiano and to slice the mushrooms. Layer these ingredients on top of the meat.

Drizzle over the lemon juice dressing and serve.

THE FLAVOUR OF RAW MEAT

Carpaccio all'albese is a traditional appetizer from Piedmont. As the name suggests the dish originated in the town of Alba in the province of Cuneo but is now popular throughout the region. The slices of veal must be extremely fresh and preferably from Fassone cattle, a breed esteemed for its very lean and tender meat. The traditional recipe involves layering the beef on a bed of lettuce and dressing it with just lemon juice, a dash of extra-virgin olive oil, garlic, salt and black pepper. There are however other variations which see the addition of Parmigiano Reggiano shavings or thinly sliced mushrooms. When in season a generous grating of black or white Alba truffle over the raw meat is also a welcome variation.

ASIAN MEATBALLS

Ingredients for approximately 15 meatballs
Preparation time 1 hour (45 minutes preparation + 15 minutes cooking)

FOR THE MEATBALLS
5 1/2 oz. (150 g) lamb
5 1/2 oz. (150 g) beef
1 tsp. (2 g) total powdered spices
  (cumin, bay, mace, clove,
  ginger, pepper)
extra-virgin olive oil
salt

FOR THE SAUCE
1 shallot
2 tsp. (10 ml) extra-virgin olive oil
1/2 garlic clove
1 bay leaf
1 sprig thyme
1 tbsp. (2 g) curry powder
1/2 apple
salt

Preparation

Chop the shallot and sweat in a frying pan with the oil, garlic, bay leaf and thyme. Add the curry and continue cooking for one minute, add the diced apple (peeled or washed and unpeeled) and cover with water. Season with salt and cook for approximately 30 minutes. Blend the mixture and sieve.

Pour the mixture back in the pan.

Remove any excess fat from the beef and lamb and dice.

Pass the meat through a mincer and season with salt, pepper and spices.

Knead the mixture thoroughly and divide into equal portions.

Use your hands to mould each portion into the shape of a large olive.

Simmer the meatballs directly in the sauce for approximately 15 minutes.

A MIXTURE OF EXOTIC FLAVOURS

In Italian cooking and European cooking in general, the English word "curry" means a blend of Indian spices. When ground in a mortar the mixture of spices turns to the colour of ochre and gives off a powerful aroma. In the Indian culinary tradition the word means a variety of blends called a "masala" which exists in dozens of variations. The classic curry blend contains black pepper, cumin, coriander, cinnamon, turmeric, cloves, ginger, nutmeg, fenugreek and chilli with the taste ranging from mild to hot depending on the amount of chilli. This spicy powder has many uses in the kitchen and can be used in risottos, pasta sauces, soups, meat dishes, especially chicken, fish dishes, especially prawns and salmon, vegetable dishes and pulse recipes. It is also an excellent ingredient when making desserts, especially chocolate-based ones.

RABBIT SALAD PINWHEELS

Ingredients for 12 pinwheels
Preparation time 13 hours 45 minutes
(45 hours preparation + 12 hours marinating + 1 hour cooking)

FOR THE DOUGH
9 oz. (250 g) all-purpose flour
1/2 cup (125 ml) milk
1 oz. (25 g) + 1 oz. (30 g) lard
1 tsp. (5 g) salt

FOR THE FILLING
1/2 rabbit
1 carrot

1/2 onion
1 celery stick
1 bay leaf
1 bunch sage
5 1/2 tbsp. (80 ml) extra-virgin olive oil
1 3/4 oz. (50 g) valerian
1 garlic clove
3-4 juniper berries
salt and pepper

Preparation

Put the onion, half the carrot (the other half is for the filling), the celery stick and bay leaf in a large pan. Cover with water and bring to the boil. Lightly season with salt and add the rabbit in one piece. Simmer for approximately one hour then leave to cool.

Once the rabbit has cooled take it out of the stock, remove the meat from the carcass and shred the meat. Wash the sage and peel the garlic. Put the rabbit meat, sage, garlic, juniper berries, pepper and extra-virgin olive oil in a sealed plastic container and place in the fridge to marinate for approximately 12 hours.

For the dough make the flour into a well on a pastry board. Add the milk, 1 oz. (25 g) of soft lard and salt. Mix the ingredients into a smooth and pliable dough. Leave the dough to rest for at least half an hour.

Use a rolling pin to roll out the dough to a thickness of 1/32 to 1/16 inch (1-2 mm) creating a rectangle of approximately 16 inches by 20 inches (40 cm by 50 cm). Spread the remainder of the soft lard on the dough and roll up the pastry to form a long narrow sausage shape. Flatten the roll slightly and cut into pieces (approximately 1 1/4 inches [3 cm]). Roll these pieces up and then roll them out with a rolling pin to make circles with a thickness of 1/32 to 1/16 inch (1-2 mm).

Cook for 2-3 minutes on each side using a griddle or non-stick frying pan.

Remove the rabbit meat from the marinade and spread it over the warm pastry circles. Wash and clean the valerian. Cut the rest of the carrot into julienne. Layer the valerian and carrot on the meat. Roll up the circles and trim to the size required.

BRESAOLA, CAPRINO GOAT'S CHEESE AND ROCKET PINWHEELS

Ingredients for 6-8 people
Preparation time 20 minutes (10 minutes preparation + 10 minutes resting)

2 oz. (60 g) sandwich loaf bread
1 1/2 oz. (45 g) fresh caprino goat's cheese
3/4 oz. (20 g) sliced bresaola
1/2 oz. (10 g) rocket
extra-virgin olive oil
salt and pepper

Preparation

Use very soft and fresh sandwich loaf bread.

Remove the crusts, spread a thin layer of goat's cheese over the bread, layer a slice of bresaola and some rocket on top and season with a pinch of salt, pepper and a drop of extra-virgin olive oil.

Roll up the bread (use a sheet of cling film to help you) to form a roulade. Place in the fridge for atleast 10 minutes to rest.

Cut the roulade into pinwheels and serve.

A LEAN AND TASTY COLD CUT

Bresaola from the Valtellina is a cold cut with Protected Geographical Indication status. It is made by salting and curing beef. The name is derived from the term "brasa" which in the local Valtellina dialect means embers. Originally bresaola was dried before curing in rooms heated by braziers burning spruce and aromatised with juniper berries, thyme and bayleaf. The first written record of domestic production of this cold cut dates back to the fifteenth century but the true origin is undoubtedly older. Bresaola is low in fat and therefore widely consumed, particularly in calorie-controlled diets. Bresaola can also be made using different tyupes of meats. Bresaola made with horsemeat is popular in Piedmont, particularly around Asti, and in Veneto around the province of Padua. Venison bresaola is produced in the province of Novara in Piedmont. The meat is marinated in a red wine-based brine before being cased, dried and cured.

LAMB KOFTA

Ingredients for 10 kebabs
Preparation time 30 minutes (20 minutes preparation + 10 minutes cooking)

10 1/2 oz. (300 g) lamb
1 tsp. (2 g) powdered cumin
1 tbsp. (1 g) fresh coriander, chopped
extra-virgin olive oil
salt and pepper

Preparation

Remove any excess fat from the lamb and dice.

Pass the meat through a mincer and season with salt, pepper, cumin and coriander.

Knead the mixture thoroughly and divide into 10 equal portions.

Use your hands to mould each portion into a sausage shape around a kebab skewer.

Cook on a hot, greased grill or alternatively, in the oven at 390°F (200°C), for approximately 10 minutes.

CARNIVAL CONFETTI

Coriander (scientific name Coriandrum sativum), *also known as Chinese parsley and cilantro, is an annual herb in the family Apiaceae just like dill, cumin, fennel and parsley. Coriander has been used as an aromatic and medicinal herb since ancient times. The Romans were particularly fond of it and used it in cooking and medicine. Pliny is quoted as saying that placing a few coriander seeds under your pillow at dawn was en excellent remedy for headaches and helped prevent the onset of fever. At the time of the Renaissance the throwing of sugar-coated coriander seeds into the air became a popular custom during festivities. The modern Italian word for confetti is "coriandoli". Later the coriander seeds were replaced by small balls of chalk which in 1875 became the small discs of paper we know today.*

WHITE MEAT KEBABS

Ingredients for 4 people
Preparation time 2 hours 40 minutes
(30 minutes preparation + 2 marinating + 10 minutes cooking)

1 1/2 oz. (40 g) chicken breast
1 1/2 oz. (40 g) guineafowl breast
1 1/2 oz. (40 g) pork loin
1 1/2 oz. (40 g) turkey breast
4 tbsp. (60 ml) white wine
1 3/4 tbsp. (25 ml) extra-virgin olive oil
1 lemon
1 bunch sage
oil to grease the grill
salt and pepper

Preparation

Cut all the meat into cubes (approximately 3/4 inch [2 cm]) and marinate in a glass bowl for approximately 2 hours with the white wine and olive oil.

Cut the lemon into small wedges. Wash and dry the sage.

Thread the different types of meat, lemon wedges and sage leaves alternately onto kebab skewers.

Cook the kebabs on a clean, greased grill for approximately ten minutes. Season with salt and pepper.

Brush the kebabs with the marinade while cooking.

A HERB TO BE HARVESTED WITH RESPECT

Sage is an aromatic herb originating in the Mediterranean and belonging to the same family as thyme and mint, Lamiaceae. The most well-known variety is Salvia officinalis which is widely used in cooking. Sage has numerous pharmaceutical properties and can be used as an antiseptic, to aid digestion, as a diuretic, painkiller, balm, to stimulate blood flow in the uterus, as a spasmodic, to treat hypoglycemia, to stimulate the production of oestrogen and to lower cholesterol. Sage was known to and appreciated by the ancient Egyptians and Romans who used to harvest the plant using a special rite. Those harvesting sage were forbidden from using iron objects, had to wear a white robe and go barefoot ensuring the feet were also very clean. Today sage is much more than just a medicinal plant. It is widely used in cooking to enhance the flavour of various meat dishes, in butter sauces to accompany stuffed pasta dishes and to exalt the taste of herb cheeses.

VEGETARIAN
DELICACIES

HERE IS AN EXCELLENT WAY OF BEING MORE ADVENTUROUS WITH VEGETABLES INSTEAD OF JUST USING THEM TO PREPARE PASTA SAUCES AND SIDE DISHES. VEGETABLES DESERVE BETTER. NO LONGER BIT-PART PLAYERS WITH A PLATE OF PASTA OR ALONGSIDE A STEAK OR A ROASTED FISH, HERE VEGETABLES PLAY A LEADING ROLE. A ROLE OF THE UTMOST IMPORTANCE.

THE IDEA OF TRANSFORMING VEGETABLES INTO APPETIZERS, THUS EXALTING THEM IN ALL THEIR FLAVOUR WITHOUT RELYING ON OTHER "NOBLER" INGREDIENTS, IS AN EXCELLENT ONE. THE VARIETY OF APPETIZING SNACKS WHICH CAN BE MADE USING VEGETABLES IS ENDLESS, WITH EACH ONE MORE TEMPTING THAN THE NEXT. WE EAT WITH OUR EYES AS WELL AS OUR PALATE. A PLETHORA OF SHAPES, COLOURS AND TASTES RANGING FROM THE MOST DELICATE TO THE MOST INTENSE. WITHOUT IGNORING HEALTHY EATING AND THE WAISTLINE. THE MINERAL SALTS, VITAMINS AND PHYTONUTRIENTS CONTAINED IN VEGETABLES ARE VITAL FOR OUR WELLBEING. THEIR LOW-CALORIE CONTENT ALSO MAKES THEM THE BEST POSSIBLE ALLY IN THE DAILY SKIRMISH WITH THE BATHROOM SCALES. FOR EXAMPLE, SUMMER VEGETABLE ROLLS, UPSIDE-DOWN SPRING ONION TARTLETS, MIXED VEGETABLE CROQUETTES, TOASTED BREAD AND TOMATO SALAD WITH TOFU AND KALAMATA OLIVES, GUACAMOLE WITH CORN CHIPS AND SUMMER VEGETABLE TABBOULEH ARE ALL DELICIOUSLY LIGHT APPETISERS WHICH ARE EASY TO DIGEST. THESE DISHES DO NOT KILL YOUR APPETITE IMMEDIATELY. INDEED THEIR SALT CONTENT AND FRAGRANCE PREPARE THE GASTRIC JUICES FOR THE FOOD TO FOLLOW. THEY ARE ALSO POPULAR WITH CHILDREN WHO OFTEN TURN UP THEIR NOSES AT THE SIMPLE MENTION OF THE WORD "VEGETABLES".

APPETZERS PREPARED WITH PULSES ARE ALSO DISHES SUITABLE FOR VEGETARIANS. DELICIOUS FALAFEL WITH YOGHURT DIP, BROAD BEAN DIP WITH CRISPY BREAD, AND CANNELLINI BEAN AND ROSEMARY HUMMUS WITH SWEET AND SOUR ONION ARE JUST THREE OF THE WONDERFUL LEGUME RECIPES IN THIS BOOK. THIS IS AN EXCELLENT OPPORTUNITY TO EAT FOODS WHICH ARE VITAL FOR A HEALTHY, NUTRITIOUS DIET WHICH IS RICH IN FIBRE. THIS COMBINATION OF PULSES AND OTHER TASTY INGREDIENTS IS THE PERFECT MOMENT TO LIVE TO EAT RATHER THAN EAT TO LIVE.

EGGS AND CHEESE ARE OFTEN ADDED TO VEGETABLE-BASED APPETISERS. THIS BOOK INCLUDES RECIPES FOR OVEN-BAKED COURGETTE AND MINT FRITTATA, PANCAKES STUFFED WITH AUBERGINE, BUFFALO MOZZARELLA AND BASIL, PEPPER STUFFED WITH FRESH GOAT'S CHEESE, FRIED MOZZARELLA SANDWICHES, CARASAU FLATBREAD MILLEFEUILLE WITH BURRATA CHEESE, TOMATOES AND BASIL-INFUSED OLIVE. IN OTHER RECIPES CHEESE AND EGGS ARE THE MAIN INGREDIENTS. THERE ARE ALSO RECIPES FOR MORE SUBSTANTIAL DISHES CONTAINING MORE PROTEIN WHERE VEGETABLES DO NOT EVEN MAKE AN APPEARANCE. THESE INCLUDE CACIOCAVALLO CHEESE MUFFINS, PUGLIA BREAD AND SCAMORZA CHEESE KEBABS, TOMME CHEESE CRACKERS, WARM CREAMED CHEESE PUFFS, AND DOUBLE-COOKED QUAIL EGGS.

TOASTED BREAD AND TOMATO SALAD
WITH TOFU AND KALAMATA OLIVES

Ingredients for 4-6 people
Preparation time 20 minutes

3 1/2 oz. (100 g) stale brown bread
1 tomato
1 cucumber
1 tbsp. capers
1 bunch basil
2 tbsp. (30 ml) extra-virgin olive oil
6 Kalamata olives
2 oz. (60 g) tofu
1/2 tsp. (3 g) salt
oregano

Preparation

Remove the crust from the bread and cut into pieces (approximately 1/4 to 2/7 inch [6-7 mm]). Toast in a frying pan or the oven at 350°F (180°C) for a few minutes.

Remove the seeds from the tomato and dice (approximately 1/5 inch [5 mm]). Peel the cucumber, remove the seeds and dice in the same way as with the tomato.

Stone the olives. Dice the tofu and olives.

Cut the capers in half and mix all the vegetables together in a bowl. Season with a pinch of salt and the oregano. Mix in the toasted bread and serve in small glasses.

Wash and dry the basil. Garnish the salad with the basil and olive oil (alternatively make a cruet of olive oil available to diners) and serve.

SOY CHEESE

Tofu, also known in the Far East as "soy cheese", is made into rectangular blocks or a smooth, velvety cream. It was first produced in China around 164 BC before becoming widespread throughout the Far East. It is made from the curds of the juice extracted from yellow soya beans. Other ingredients are added depending on the final consistency required. The range of other ingredients includes calcium chloride, magnesium chloride, glucono delta-lactone (a natural organic acid) and just plain old lemon juice. Tofu, rich in protein and with a neutral odour and taste, is usually sold au naturel but can also be found aromatised with garlic, basil or tomato. The flavour of sweet versions can be enhanced by coconut, almonds or mango. It is also available smoked or preserved in brine or cooked on a grill or fried.

WARM CREAMED CHEESE PUFFS

Ingredients for 25 puffs
Preparation time 55 minutes (40 minutes preparation + 15 minutes cooking)

FOR THE PUFFS
6 3/4 tbsp. (100 ml) water
1 3/4 oz. (50 g) butter
2 oz. (60 g) all-purpose flour
2 eggs
salt

FOR THE CREAMED CHEESE
1 cup (250 ml) milk
1 egg
3 egg yolks
1/2 oz. (10 g) all-purpose flour
1/2 oz. (15 g) butter
2 oz. (60 g) Parmigiano Reggiano
cheese, grated
salt

Preparation

To make the puffs boil the water in a pan with the salt and butter. Add the flour and cook until the mixture no longer sticks to the side of the pan.

Remove from the heat and add the eggs one at a time, mixing thoroughly. Line a baking tray with greaseproof paper and mould the puffs on the tray using a piping bag. Bake the puffs in the oven at 375°F (190°C) for approximately 15 minutes.

To make the creamed Parmigiano Reggiano, beat the egg and egg yolks with the salt in a pan. Boil the milk in a separate pan then add the flour and milk to the beaten egg mixture.

Bring to the boil and simmer for 2-3 minutes. Remove from the heat and add the cheese and butter.

Stuff the puffs with the creamed Parmigiano Reggiano using a piping bag. Warm the puffs in the hot oven for a few minutes and serve.

A LIGHT SHELL FOR A GLUTTONOUS FILLING

Pastry puffs (bignè in Italian from the French beignet) are small round pastries. They can be stuffed with various fillings, both sweet and savory, as is the case in this recipe using creamed Parmigiano Reggiano. The neutrally-tasting dough, known as choux pastry, is made from water, butter, flour and egg. The pastry is moulded into small balls on a baking tray using a piping bag. As they cook the puffs expand to become hollow in the middle making them ready for filling. Their size can vary from from 1 to 2 1/2 inches (3-6 cm) to 4 to 5 inches (10-12 cm). Savoury pastry puffs are usually smaller than sweet ones because they are intended to be eaten as part of a buffet or as an accompaniment to an aperitif.

MEDITERRANEAN SAVORY CAKE

Ingredients for 6-8 people
Preparation time 1 hour 45 minutes
(1 hour 20 minutes preparation + 25 minutes cooking)

4 tsp. (20 ml) extra-virgin olive oil
2 eggs
4 1/2 tbsp. (65 ml) milk
4 3/4 oz. (135 g) all-purpose flour
1 1/2 oz. (40 g) Parmigiano Reggiano cheese, grated
2 tomatoes
2 tsp. (11 g) baking powder
oregano
salt and pepper

Preparation

Put the tomatoes in boiling water for a few seconds. Leave to cool in cold water, peel, cut into quarters and remove the seeds. Season with a pinch of salt, pepper, and oregano and cook in the oven at 180-190°F (80-90°C) for approximately one hour.

Beat the eggs in a bowl with the milk and extra-virgin olive oil. Season with salt and pepper.

Mix the flour with the baking powder and add together with the Parmigiano Reggiano and the tomatoes cut into strips.

Mix all the ingredients without overdoing it.

Line a cake tin with greaseproof paper and pour in the mixture until it is three quarters full. Bake in the oven at 350°F (180°C) for approximately 25 minutes.

Leave to cool and then cut into bite-size pieces.

FROM THE VEGETABLE GARDEN TO THE MEDICINE CABINET

Oregano (scientific name: Origanum vulgare) is an aromatic plant widely used in Mediterranean cooking and as a medicinal herb. Not only does it contain phenols, vitamins and mineral salts such as iron, potassium, calcium and manganese, it is also one of the most powerful antibiotics made available to us by nature. Oregano has anti-inflammatory, antiseptic and antispasmodic properties which are useful in preventing mainly respiratory illnesses. This medicinal plant can be used as a painkiller and antioxidant, to combat cellulite and even, according to recent research, to fight cancer thanks to a substance it contains which induces carcinogenic cells to destroy themselves. From the vegetable garden to the medicine cabinet.

AUBERGINE CAVIAR WITH PASTRY PUFFS

Ingredients for 4 people
Preparation time 55 minutes-1 hour and 5 minutes
(15 minutes preparation + 40-50 minutes cooking)

FOR THE AUBERGINE CAVIAR
1 aubergine (approx. 10 1/2 oz / 300 g)
1 garlic clove
3-4 mint leaves
3 1/2 tbsp. (50 ml) extra-virgin olive oil
salt and pepper

FOR THE PASTRY PUFFS
3 1/2 oz. (100 g) puff pastry
1 1/2 oz. (40 g) Parmigiano Reggiano cheese, grated

Preparation

Wash and dry the aubergine. Peel the garlic and cut into sticks. Use a knife to make small holes in the skin of the aubergine and place the garlic in the holes.

Wrap the aubergine in tin foil and cook in the oven at 350°F (180°C) for approximately 30-40 minutes until the aubergine is very soft.

In the meantime prepare the pastry puffs.

Roll the puff pastry into a rectangle to a thickness of approximately 1/16 inch (2 mm). Use a pastry brush to wet the surface using water.

Cover the surface with the grated Parmigiano Reggiano and roll up the pastry. Place in the fridge for a few minutes to cool. Remove from the fridge and cut the roulade into slices with a thickness of 1/16 inch (2 mm). Flatten the slices using a rolling pin.

Place the pastry puffs on a baking tray lined with greaseproof paper. Cook in the oven at 350-390°F (180-200°C) for approximately 10 minutes.

When the aubergine is cooked use a spoon to remove the flesh. Place the aubergine in a blender and mix with the washed and dried mint leaves. When the mixture has turned into a puree, add the extra-virgin olive oil and season with salt and pepper.

Serve the aubergine caviar accompanied by the pastry puffs.

UNHEALTHY APPLES

Aubergines are the fruit of a plant in the nightshade family (scientific name Solanum melongena). The plant and fruit bear the same name. Originally from India the plant was brought to Europe at the beginning of the 4th century by Arabs. In Italy it was originally called "petonciana", then "melangiana" before becoming the "melanzana" of today. The modern Italian word derives from "mela non sana" – or unhealthy apple – because unlike apples aubergines must be cooked before eating.

FILO PASTRY BASKETS WITH TOMME CHEESE, CELERY AND WALNUTS

Ingredients for 10 baskets
Preparation time 25 minutes (15 minutes preparation + 10 minutes cooking)

3 sheets filo pastry (3/4 oz.-20 g)
2 tbsp. (30 ml) extra-virgin olive oil
7 oz. (200 g) tomme cheese
3 1/2 oz. (100 g) celery
1 1/2 oz. (40 g) shelled walnuts
1 3/4 tbsp. (25 ml) walnut oil
salt and pepper

Preparation

Brush the sheets of filo pastry with the olive oil and cut into 10 squares. Place the squares in small moulds and bake in the oven at 350°F (180°C) for approximately 10 minutes. Leave to cool.

In the meantime, remove the crust from the tomme and cut into small pieces. Wash and chop the celery. Mix these ingredients together and add some chopped walnuts. Season with a pinch of pepper, salt and the walnut oil.

Fill the filo pastry baskets with the cheese mixture and serve.

A SALAD MIRACLE-WORKER

Celery (scientific name Apium graveolens) *is a plant variety of the Apiaceae family. Originally from the Mediterranean, it has been noted for its medicinal properties since ancient times. Two main varieties are used in the kitchen: green celery used mainly to give flavour to mirepoix and salads and celeriac which has a milder taste and is ideal when used as a main ingredient. It is the long leaf stalks of celery and the root of the celeriac which are used in cooking. Celery has many hidden properties. Not only does it help to keep you in trim – it's said that celery contains so few calories you need more of them to eat it – it's also very good for your health. Celery fibre helps to reduce triglyceride and cholesterol levels in the blood and assists the digestive process. Other phytochemicals assist in the treatment of high blood pressure. That's not all. Celery also has diuretic, detoxification and anti-inflammatory properties.*

GUACAMOLE WITH CORN CHIPS

Ingredients for 4 people
Preparation time 1 hour 45 minutes (45 minutes preparation + 1 hour cooking)

FOR THE GUACAMOLE
1 avocado
1 tsp. (6 g) white onion, chopped
1/2 fresh chilli
1/4 lime
1 tomato
salt

FOR THE CORN CHIPS
1 cup (250 ml) water
2 oz. (60 g) maize flour
salt

Preparation

Sprinkle the maize flour into the boiling salted water. Cook for approximately 1/2 hour stirring frequently with a wooden spoon.

When the polenta is cooked spread a thin layer between two pieces of greaseproof paper or silicone. Leave to cool, remove the top piece of greaseproof paper or silicone and use the tip of a small knife to cut the polenta into the shapes required.

Place the corn chips in the oven at 250°F (120°C) for at least an hour.

For the guacamole, cut the avocado in half, remove the stone and use a spoon to remove the flesh.

Mash or coarsely dice the flesh, add the chopped onion, chopped chilli pepper, lime juice and a pinch of salt.

Store in the fridge until ready to serve and then add the chopped tomato at the last minute.

Serve with the corn chips.

THE MOST VALUABLE FRUIT FOR GOOD HEALTH

Avocados are the fleshy fruit of a tropical plant belonging to the laurel family originating in Central America, Mexico and the Andes. The fruit was first discovered by Europeans during the Spanish conquest of the Americas. Avocados are highly nutritious thanks to their rich fat content which makes them very high in calories. They are an excellent source of monounsaturated fats, mineral salts including potassium and magnesium, folic acid and vitamin E, a powerful anti-oxidant. The avocado is the most valuable fruit to ensure good health. This is also because the combination of avocado and other ingredients helps us to absorb better the fat-soluble nutrients in foodstuffs. For example some diced avocado mixed with salad allows us to absorb 4 times as much alpha-carotene found in lettuce and 14 times as much beta-carotene found in carrots.

HUMMUS WITH WARM FLATBREAD

Ingredients for 4 people
Preparation time 13 hours 45 minutes
(12 hours soaking + 45 minutes preparation + 1 hour cooking)

FOR THE HUMMUS
3 1/2 oz. (100 g) chickpeas
6 3/4 tbsp. (100 ml) extra-virgin olive oil
2 tbsp. (30 g) sesame seeds
juice of 1/2 lemon
1/2 garlic clove
salt and pepper

FOR THE FLATBREAD
4 1/2 oz. (125 g) flour
3/4 oz. (20 g) lard
1/2 tsp. (3 g) salt
1 tsp. (6 g) baking powder
4 tbsp. (60 ml) milk

Preparation

Soak the chickpeas in cold water overnight.

Cook the chickpeas in unsalted boiling water for approximately one hour.

In the meantime, prepare the hummus. Toast the sesame seeds in a frying pan over a medium heat. Blend into a paste by adding a drop of oil if necessary.

Drain the chickpeas, remove the skins and place them in a food processor with half the olive oil, lemon juice, garlic, sesame seed paste, salt and pepper. Blend all the ingredients, if necessary by adding a small amount of the chickpea water.

For the flatbread, mix all the ingredients together to make a smooth and homogenous dough. Wrap in cling film and place in the fridge for an hour.

Divide the dough into two and roll each half using a rolling pin to make two circles with a thickness of approximately 1/16 inch (2 mm). Use a fork to prick holes in the dough.

Cook the circles for 2-3 minutes on both sides over a high heat using a griddle or non-stick frying pan.

Drizzle the remaining olive oil over the hummus and serve with hot flatbread.

CHICKPEAS IN THE KITCHEN

After beans and soya beans, chickpeas (scientific name Cicer arietinum) are the world's most widely-diffused pulse and have been eaten since ancient times. Chickpeas can be used in salads either on their own or with other vegetables. They must be soaked for 12-16 hours and then cooked in lightly salted boiling water flavoured with bay leaf, rosemary or sage. They can also be used for soups, pasta sauces and as the main ingredient in classic Italian foods such as the "farinata" or "cecina" flatbreads originating in Liguria and Tuscany. Chickpeas are also the basic ingredient of hummus, the traditional Middle Eastern dip.

CANNELLINI BEAN AND ROSEMARY HUMMUS WITH SWEET AND SOUR ONION

Ingredients for 4-6 people
Preparation time 13 hours 30 minutes
(30 hours preparation + 12 hours soaking + 1 hour cooking)

3 1/2 oz. (100 g) cannellini beans
1 oz. (30 g) onion
1 oz. (30 g) carrot
1 oz. (30 g) celery
1/2 bay leaf
4 tsp. (20 ml) extra-virgin olive oil
5 1/2 oz. (150 g) red onion
3/4 cup (200 ml) wine vinegar
1 oz. (30 g) brown sugar
salt and pepper
2 sprigs rosemary

Preparation

Soak the cannellini beans in cold water for 12 hours.

Drain and place in a large pan of boiling water with the onion, carrot, celery and half bay leaf. Simmer for approximately one hour or until the beans are soft. Season with salt at the end of cooking.

In the meantime slice the red onion and heat in a pan with the vinegar, a pinch of salt and the brown sugar. When the mixture starts to boil, remove from the heat and pour off the liquid.

When the beans are cooked, drain and blend in a food processor with the olive oil and some chopped rosemary (approximately half a sprig). Season to taste with salt and pepper and if necessary dilute with a some of the water used to cook the beans.

Spoon the hummus into single-serving glasses, add some onion and garnish with rosemary, some freshly-ground black pepper and a drop of olive oil.

A DELICATE PULSE

Cannellini beans are one of the many types of bean imported into Europe from Central America following the discovery of the new world. They are widely used in Italian cooking. Cannellini beans are especially popular in Tuscany where they are used in traditional recipes such as "fagioli all'uccelletto", a side dish of beans in tomato sauce served with meat courses and particularly sausages. These dishes are delicious yet quick and easy to prepare. Cannellini beans are excellent in soups, pureed and transformed into a savoury mousse. They also make very tasty pasta sauces especially when combined with fish.

BROAD BEAN DIP WITH CRISPY BREAD

Ingredients for 4 people
Preparation time 1 hour (20 minutes preparation + 40 minutes cooking)

3/4 oz. (20 g) onion
3 1/2 oz. (100 g) broad beans (fresh or frozen)
4 tsp. (20 ml) extra-virgin olive oil
3 1/2 oz. (100 g) stale bread
2 cups (500 ml) vegetable stock
salt

Preparation

Cook the broad beans in boiling salted water, drain, leave to cool and remove the outer membrane from the beans.

Chop the onion and sweat in a pan with a dash of olive oil. Add the broad beans and continue cooking for a few minutes. Cover with the vegetable stock. Season with salt and cook for approximately half an hour. When cooked blend the beans in a food processor to obtain a dense, velvet liquid.

Thinly slice half the bread and place in the oven at 350°F (180°C) to dry out for a few minutes.

Break the rest of the bread into crumbs and sauté in a frying pan with the remaining olive oil until crispy.

Garnish with the breadcrumbs, a drizzle of olive oil and serve with the crispy pieces of bread.

TASTY, NUTRITIOUS AND LOW IN CALORIES

The broad bean (scientific name Vicia faba) is a plant in the family Fabaceae. Originally from Asia Minor the fruit, or bean, of the plant is flat, oval, wide and fleshy with a yellow brown colour. The calorie content of broad beans is the lowest of all pulses. They are also rich in protein, minerals such as iron, potassium, magnesium, copper, and selenium and vitamin C. Broad beans are mainly used in Central and Southern Italian cooking, They can be eaten raw, on their own or together with cheese and cold cuts, or dried and then cooked. The most common use is to purée the beans and serve them alongside vegetables with a bitter taste such as chicory.

FALAFEL WITH YOGURT DIP

Ingredients for 6-8 people
Preparation time 12 hours 45-50 minutes
(30 minutes preparation + 12 hours soaking + 15-20 minutes cooking)

FOR THE FALAFEL
5 1/2 oz. (150 g) dried chickpeas
3/4 oz. (20 g) onion
1/2 tsp. (1 g) cumin
2 tbsp. (30 ml) extra-virgin olive oil
1 3/4 oz. (50 g) sesame seeds (optional)
salt and pepper

FOR THE DIP
1 cup (250 ml) Greek yogurt
2 tsp. (10 ml) extra-virgin olive oil
salt and pepper

Preparation

Rinse the chickpeas and leave to soak in lots of water for at least 12 hours.

Drain well and blend in a food processor with a pinch of salt and pepper, the onion and a drop of olive oil.

Grind the cumin finely and add to the chickpeas.

Mould the mixture into small flattened balls and coat in sesame seeds (optional).

Grease a baking tray with the remaining olive oil and cook in the oven at 350°F (180°C) for approximately 15-20 minutes.

Mix the yoghurt and olive oil with a pinch of salt and pepper.

Serve the falafel accompanied by the yoghurt dip.

SEEDS WITH A STRONG AND WARM FRAGRANCE

Cumin (scientific name Cuminum cyminum) is a flowering plant in the family Apiaceae, native from the east Mediterranean to India. Cumin seeds are similar dill and fennel seeds but are slightly smaller and darker in colour. False etymology places the origin of the word cumin in the Persian city of Kerman which seems to have been the largest cumin producing site in the whole of Persia. The expression "taking cumin to Kerman" even became an idiom meaning to do something pointless. Used since ancient times thanks to its strong and warm aroma, but also for its medicinal properties – cumin seeds were found at the archaeological site of Tell ed-Der in Iraq and dated to the second millennium BC, – today cumin is mainly used in Indian, Middle Eastern, North African, Cuban and Mexican cooking.

MIXED VEGETABLE CROQUETTES

Ingredients for 15 small croquettes
Preparation time 40 minutes (30 minutes preparation + 10 minutes cooking)

9 oz. (250 g) courgette
10 1/2 oz. (300 g) potato
1 3/4 tbsp. (25 ml) extra-virgin olive oil
1 garlic clove
salt and pepper

Preparation

Boil the potatoes without peeling them for approximately 10 minutes.

Leave to cool, peel and shred using a large-hole grater.

In the meantime wash the courgette, slice lengthways and then across to obtain a julienne cut.

Peel the garlic. Heat the oil in a pan and add the garlic. Sauté for approximately one minute, remove the garlic and add the courgettes. Sauté for a few seconds then add the potatoes.

Season with salt and pepper and cook for a few minutes on a high heat stirring all the time.

Mould the mixture into small croquettes, place them on a baking tray lined with greaseproof paper and cook in the oven at 350°F (180°C) for approximately 10 minutes.

A LIGHT TASTE

The courgette is the young fruit of the Cucurbita pepo plant. It is harvested when it reaches a length of 8 to 10 inches (20-25 cm), that is to say before it matures and turns into a pumpkin. Fresh courgettes are easily distinguishable by their smooth taut skin, bright green colour and barely discernible down. Courgettes are rich in folate, potassium, manganese and vitamin A. These nutrients are exploited to the full when the vegetable is freshly picked. A high water content means that courgettes have a low-calorie content. They are tasty but light making them an ideal side dish. They can be finely sliced and eaten raw with a dressing of extra-virgin olive oil, salt and mint leaves. Alternatively they can be grilled, cooked on the stove with garlic and parsley or sage and lemon and even transformed into a gratin to be baked in the oven. Courgettes are also delicious when served as an appetiser. Who can resist courgette sticks coated in batter and fried? They also make an excellent light pasta sauce whether prepared on their own or with fish.

POTATO CROCKETS

Ingredients for 6 people
Preparation time 45 minutes (40 minutes preparation + 5 minutes cooking)

9 oz. (250 g) potato
2 eggs
3/4 oz. (20 g) butter
1 oz. (30 g) Parmigiano Reggiano cheese, grated
1 oz. (30 g) almonds
1 oz. (30 g) peanuts
1 oz. (30 g) hazelnuts
1 oz. (30 g) pistachio nuts
all-purpose flour
vegetable oil
nutmeg
salt

Preparation

Chop all the nuts.

Wash the potatoes and cook in their skins in lightly salted boiling water. When cooked mash the po-tatoes in a bowl.

Add an egg yolk, the soft butter, grated Parmigiano Reggiano, a pinch of nutmeg and season with salt to taste.

Mould the potatoes into crockets, coat them in flour, the remaining beaten eggs and then the chopped nuts.

Fry the crockets in lots of very hot oil, drain on kitchen roll and season with salt.

THE SPITEFUL INVENTION OF FRENCH FRIES

The idea of finely slicing potatoes and frying them first came to the American chef, George Crum in 1853 when he was working at the Moon Lake Lodge Resort restaurant in New York. This wasn't a culinary experiment or a flash of gastronomic creativity. No, not at all. It was an attempt to spite a demanding customer. The man in question, responsible for the tastiest culinary invention of the last two hundred years, sent a plate of boiled potatoes back to the kitchen three times claiming they had been chopped into pieces which were too small. The chef lost patience and so sliced them into very thin pieces before frying them in extremely hot oil. He was sure this would be the final straw for the customer who would be left with little choice but to walk out. Wishful thinking! The insatiable customer declared them delicious! Word of mouth rapidly spread and before long French fries were being produced on an industrial scale throughout the world.

UPSIDE-DOWN SPRING ONION TARTLETS

Ingredients for 12 tartlets
Preparation time 50 minutes (30 minutes preparation + 20 minutes cooking)

5 1/2 oz. (150 g) puff pastry
12 spring onions
1 tsp. (5 ml) extra-virgin olive oil
3/4 oz. (20 g) brown sugar
salt and pepper

Preparation

Clean the spring onions, remove the green part and cut them in half lengthways.

Heat the oil in a pan, add the spring onions, season with salt and pepper and brown on both sides. Sprinkle over the brown sugar and leave to caramelise over a medium heat making sure the onions do not burn.

Transfer the onions and caramelised base to small silicone tartlet moulds placing two halves in each mould.

Roll out the pastry to a thickness of approximately 1/16 inch (1.5 mm) and use a pastry cutter to make 12 circles slightly larger than the moulds. Use a fork to prick holes in the circles and place them over the onions. make sure the pastry is tucked in well.

Bake in the oven at 350°F (180°C) for approximately 20 minutes.

Remove the tartlets from the moulds and serve warm or at room temperature.

TASTY, NUTRITIOUS AND HEALTHY

Spring onions are the roots of onions which have not yet fully formed and are highly esteemed in cooking due to their versatility. They are excellent eaten raw, for example thinly sliced and added to a nice salad. They are also a tasty ingredient when used as the base for both simple and more complicated recipes. White spring onions have a strong flavour whereas the red variety is decidedly milder. Spring onions are packed full of nutrients including vitamins and mineral salts. They also aid digestion and act as a detoxification agent. They also help to control blood glycaemia, cholesterol and triglyceride levels.

PANCAKES STUFFED WITH AUBERGINE, BUFFALO MOZZARELLA AND BASIL

Ingredients for 6-8 people
Preparation time 1 hour 55 minutes
(45 minutes preparation + 1 hour resting + 10 minutes cooking)

FOR THE PANCAKES
3/4 cup (200 ml) milk
3 oz. (85 g) all-purpose flour
1/2 oz. (15 g) butter
2 eggs
salt

4 1/2 oz. (125 g) buffalo mozzarella
1 3/4 oz. (50 g) cherry tomatoes
5-6 basil leaves
1 leek (only the green part)
extra-virgin olive oil
salt and pepper

FOR THE FILLING
9 oz. (250 g) aubergine

FOR THE GRATIN
3/4 oz. (20 g) butter

Preparation

Whisk the eggs with the milk, flour and salt. Add the melted butter and leave to rest in the fridge for one hour.

Wash, dry, clean and dice the aubergine. Put the aubergine in a colander, lightly season with salt and leave for half an hour to release the water from the vegetable. Grease a non-stick frying pan (approx 5.5 inches diameter [14 cm]) and spoon in a small ladle of pancake mixture. As soon as one side is cooked flip the pancake over onto the other side. Repeat until the pancake mixture is finished.

Wash the leek, blanch the green part for 2-3 minutes, leave to cool in ice-cold water and cut into lengthways strips.

Sauté the aubergine pieces in a frying pan with the extra-virgin olive oil and drain onto kitchen roll.

Wash the cherry tomatoes and cut into quarters. Wash and dry the basil. Put the aubergine in a bowl with the cherry tomatoes, chopped mozzarella and torn basil leaves. Mix all the ingredients together and season to taste with salt and pepper.

Spoon the mixture into the middle of the pancakes and lift the outer edge up and inwards to form a bag-like shape. Use the strips of leek to tie up the top of pancakes.

Place the pancakes in a greased roasting tin and put a few knobs of butter on top.

Cook in the oven at 350°F (180°C) for approximately 10 minutes.

A DIVINE HERB

Every gourmet worth their salt has basil in their kitchen. This aromatic and medicinal herb was originally cultivated in tropical Asia before being imported to Europe via the Middle East. It is widely grown in Southern France and throughout Italy. In India basil is considered a sacred plant able to cure many illnesses and open the gates of heaven when the time comes. Lakshmi, Hindu Goddess of wealth, love and prosperity as well as the wife of Vishnu, is often associated with basil.

FOCACCIA BREAD

Ingredients for 4 people
Preparation time 2 hours 10 minutes
(15 minutes preparation + 1 hour 30 minutes proving + 25 minutes baking)

FOR THE DOUGH
1.1 lb (500 g) all-purpose flour
9 fl. oz. (270 ml) water
2 tsp. (10 g) malt (or honey)
8 tsp. (40 ml) extra-virgin olive oil
2 tbsp. (10 g) yeast
2 tbsp.(10 g) salt

FOR THE BRINE
6 3/4 tbsp. (100 ml) water
3 1/2 tbsp. (50 ml) extra-virgin olive oil
3 tsp. (14 g) salt

Preparation

Make the flour into a well on a pastry board. Add the malt (or honey). Dissolve the yeast in the water and slowly add the mixture to the flour. Add the oil and finally the salt. Mix the ingredients into a smooth and pliable dough.

Cover the dough with cling film and leave to prove for approximately 30 minutes in warm and humid place.

Grease a baking tray and spread the dough carefully in the tray using your fingertips. Use your fingers to make small wells in the surface of the dough to catch the brine emulsion. Put the water, extra-virgin olive oil and salt into a bowl and whisk into an emulsion. Drizzle the emulsion over the dough.

Leave the dough to prove for another hour then bake in the oven at 400-425°F (200-220°C) for approximately 25 minutes.

Allow to cool and cut into large squares.

A DAILY PLEASURE FROM BREAKFAST TO EVENING APERITIF

Genoa-style focaccia bread (known as "a fugàssa" in Genoese dialect) is a speciality of Ligurian cooking. It is a type of seasoned flatbread. Focaccia is two centimeters high and acquires its distinctive flavour because it is brushed with a special dressing of extra-virgin olive oil, water and rock salt before the final proving process begins. In Genoa it is mainly eaten at breakfast time dipped into milky coffee, as a mid-morning snack or as an appetiser to accompany a nice glass of white wine. The most common variant is made with a topping of finely sliced white onions. Other versions include adding olives or rosemary to the dough before baking.

FRIED CHEESE FONDUE

Ingredients for 4 people
Preparation time 1 hour 2-3 minutes (1 hour preparation + 2-3 minutes cooking)

FOR THE FONDUE
7 oz. (200 g) fontina cheese
2/3 cup (150 ml) milk
1 1/4 oz. (35 g) butter
1 1/4 oz. (35 g) all-purpose flour
salt

FOR THE BREADCRUMB COATING
1 3/4 oz. (50 g) flour
2 eggs
3 1/2 oz. (100 g) breadcrumbs

vegetable oil

Preparation

Melt the butter in a pan, add the flour and cook for a couple of minutes but do not brown.

Add the milk, bring to the boil and cook for one or two minutes. Leave to cool slightly and add the finely diced fontina. If necessary season with salt.

Grease a plate using a small amount of oil, spread the fondue mix on the plate and allow to cool. Cut into regular shapes (round, square or diamond), coat in flour, beaten eggs and then breadcrumbs.

Repeat this operation to obtain a double coating of breadcrumbs.

Fry in lots of very hot oil, drain on kitchen roll and serve the fried fondue piping hot.

A DISH FIT FOR KING

Fondue is a dish based on fontina cheese from the Aosta Valley. It is widely consumed in that region, Piedmont, Switzerland and the Savoy region of France. The origins of this speciality are unclear: Anthelme Brillat-Savarin suggests a Swiss origin but others claim the dish was first made in Turin when the city was under the control of Savoy. In 1854, Giovanni Vialardi, chef to kings Charles Albert and Victor Emanuel II, included this tasty recipe in his Treatise of Modern Cookery and Patisserie. Pellegrino Artusi also talked about fondue in his famous work The Science of Cooking and the Art of Fine Dining published in 1891. He even classified it as one of the top ten tastiest dishes in the Italian culinary repertoire. A dish fit for a king made using cheese with a proven aristocratic culinary tradition.

OVEN-BAKED COURGETTE AND MINT FRITTATA

Ingredients for 4 people
Preparation time 30 minutes (15 minutes preparation + 15 minutes cooking)

4 eggs
9 oz. (250 g) courgette
1 3/4 tbsp. (25 ml) extra-virgin olive oil
4-5 fresh mint leaves
salt

Preparation

Clean and wash the courgettes, remove the seeds and cut into small cubes (approximately 1/5 inch [5 mm]).

Wash, dry and chop the mint leaves.

Heat two thirds of the olive oil in a frying pan, add the courgettes and cook for 2-3. Lightly season with salt.

Beat the eggs in a bowl, add the chopped mint, a pinch of salt and mix with the cooked courgettes.

Pour the mixture into greased metal or silicone moulds and bake in the oven at 300°F (150°C) for approximately 13-15 minutes.

FRESHLY LAID OR MATURE?

Chicken eggs are used in cooking comprehensively all over the world. They are versatile, tasty, easy to digest, nutritious and cheap. One of the ways to assess the quality of an egg is by its freshness; the fresher the better. A quick test to identify the age of an egg is to place it in a bowl of water. If the egg sinks then it's fresh but if it floats then it's mature because the ageing process causes the formation of air inside the egg. In China however mature eggs are a delicacy and even eaten when years old. Yes, years. The eggs are preserved for a few months in a mixture of wood ash, salt, lime and clay. The result is an egg which lasts for ages!

TOMATO JELLY

Ingredients for 12 jelly portions
Preparation time 1 hour + 31 minutes
(1 hour and 30 minutes preparation + 1 minute cooking)

8 3/4 oz. (250 g) chopped tomatoes
3-4 basil leaves
1 tsp. (3-5 g) agar-agar
1 garlic clove
salt and pepper

Preparation

Wash the basil, peel and dry the garlic and place them in the chopped tomatoes. Leave the mixture to marinate in the fridge for an hour.

Remove the garlic clove and basil leaves and pass the chopped tomatoes through a sieve. Season with salt and pepper.

Pour into a small pan, add the agar-agar (if you wish vary the quantity to obtain a firmer or softer jelly) and cook for 1 minute on a low heat using a whisk to mix.

Pour the tomato jelly into round silicone moulds and allow to cool.

Remove the jelly from the moulds, skewer the portions with cocktail sticks and serve.

GELATINE? NO, ALGAE

Agar-agar, also called "kanten" by the Japanese, is a naturally occurring gelatine derived from various types of red algae. It is used to make gelatine for savoury and sweet recipes. It is used as a vegetarian and vegan substitute for classic gelatine. This was originally obtained from the bladders of sturgeon or from the cartilage of similar types of fish. Today the most common source is pork rind as well as beef and pork bones and cartilage. Gelatine made from agar-agar is completely of vegetable origin and has a weak taste which does not alter the flavour of other ingredients in recipes. It has a fairly solid consistency due to its excellent thickening properties. Rich in mucilage and carrageenan, a jelly-like substance also known as alginate, agar-agar is rich in mineral salts, especially iodine.

SUNFLOWER SEED BREADSTICKS

Ingredients for 25 breadsticks
Preparation time 1 hour 32-34 minutes
(20 minutes preparation + 1 hour standing + 12-14 minutes cooking)

3 1/2 oz. (100 g) butter
1 3/4 oz. (50 g) Parmigiano Reggiano cheese, grated
1 oz. (30 g) almonds
2 oz. (60 g) all-purpose flour
8 tsp. (40 g) potato flour
1 3/4 oz. (50 g) sunflower seeds
1 egg
1 egg white
nutmeg
salt

Preparation

Use a blender to chop the almonds together with the flour. Add the potato flour, some grated nutmeg and a pinch of salt.

Mix the softened butter (room temperature) with the egg. Add the grated Parmigiano Reggiano, the flour and almond mixture and a third of the sunflower seeds. Wrap the dough in cling film and leave to stand in the fridge for at least an hour.

Use a rolling pin to roll the dough into a rectangle with a thickness of 1/4 to 2/7 inch (6-7 mm).

Brush the surface with slightly whisked egg white and then sprinkle over the remaining sunflower seeds. Pres the seeds down slightly to make them stick.

Cut the dough into sticks with width of 2/7 to 1/3 inch (7-8 mm) and length of ten centimeters.

Line a baking tray with greaseproof paper, put the dough sticks on top and bake in the oven at 350°F (180°C) for approximately 12-14 minutes.

SEEDS OF WELLBEING

Sunflower seeds may be small but like other oily seeds they are a treasure trove of nutrients. They can be considered a genuine food supplement thanks to their numerous health benefits. They contain essential fatty acids, specifically folic acid and linoleic acid, vitamins E and B as well as numerous mineral salts including iron, zinc, phosphorous, magnesium and potassium. They have many varied uses in the kitchen. Au naturel or lightly toasted they can be eaten as a healthy snack or added to muesli for a healthy breakfast or to salads. They can be used as a sauce for pasta or rice or in soups. They can also be added to fruit salad, dough and any other homemade breads.

SUMMER VEGETABLE TABBOULEH

Ingredients for 4 people
Preparation time 45 minutes
(30 minutes preparation + 10 minutes cooking + 5 minutes resting)

4 1/2 oz. (125 g) bulgur wheat, pre-cooked
1 3/4 oz. (50 g) broad beans
1 1/4 oz. (35 g) peas
1 3/4 oz. (50 g) red and yellow peppers
3 1/2 oz. (100 g) carrot
3 1/2 oz. (100 g) courgette
2 tbsp. (30 ml) extra-virgin olive oil
salt

Preparation

Place the bulgur wheat in a pan with a quantity of water equal to twice it's weight and a pinch of salt.

Bring to the boil, cover, simmer for 10 minutes then remove from the heat and leave to rest for 5 minutes.

Add a dash of olive oil and fluff up the bulgur wheat using a fork.

Clean and wash all the vegetables and dice into 1/32 to 1/16 inch (1-2 mm) pieces.

Sauté the remaining vegetables separately in a frying pan in the remaining olive oil making sure they remain al dente. Blanch the peas and broad beans in boiling water and remove the skins from the latter.

Add the vegetables to the fluffed up bulgur wheat, season with salt to taste and serve in small individual glasses.

GOLDEN TURKISH GRAIN

Burghul, originally from Turkey but consumed widely throughout the Middle East, is a cereal food made from the groats of several different wheat species, most often from durum wheat. The groats are steamed, dried and then milled to different sizes with larger grains used to make soups and hot meals and the smaller ones used for salads and cold dishes. Burghul contains lots of nutrients and is an excellent source of fibre, vitamin B, phosphorous, potassium and iron. It also fills you up without having to eat too much. Therefore burghul is light, nutritious and satisfying. An ideal accompaniment to an aperitif.

VENERE RICE SALAD WITH HALF-CANDIED
CHERRY TOMATOES AND BUFFALO MOZZARELLA

Ingredients for 4 people
Preparation time 1 hour 30 minutes (1 hour and 30 minutes preparation)

4 1/4 oz. (120 g) venere rice
3 1/2 oz. (100 g) buffalo mozzarella
3 1/2 tbsp. (50 ml) extra-virgin olive oil
5 1/2 oz. (150 g) Pachino cherry tomatoes
2 tsp. (10 g) sugar
1 garlic clove
1 sprig thyme
1 bunch basil
salt and pepper

Preparation

Wash the cherry tomatoes and cut them in half. Peel the garlic and cut into slices. Mix the tomatoes with the garlic, thyme leaves, salt, pepper, sugar and a dash of olive oil. Cook in the oven at 190-210°F (90-100°C) for approximately one hour.

In the meantime cook the venere rice in boiling salted water and drain when al dente (approximately 30 minutes).

Prepare the basil-infused oil. Wash the basil and blanch in boiling water for 30 seconds. Drain and leave to cool in ice-cold water. Blend with half of the extra-virgin olive oil.

Break up the mozzarella by hand and mix with the rice and cherry tomatoes. Add the remaining olive oil and season to taste with salt and pepper.

Serve the rice salad warm or cold in small bowls and garnish with the basil-infused olive oil.

BLACK, WHOLEGRAIN, FRAGRANT

Venere rice, an Italian rice first produced in Vercelli in 1997, is a cross between an Asian variety of black rice and a variety from the Po valley. Black rice has existed for a considerable period of time in China and is widely esteemed. Not for nothing cultivation of black rice is reserved for the well-off. It is also given to expectant mothers and the sick due to its wealth of protein and mineral salts, specifically iron, manganese and selenium. Venere rice consists of small, aromatic, ebony grains with a fragrance – which becomes gradually more intense during the cooking process – reminiscent of freshly baked bread. It is a wholegrain rice and therefore rich in fibre. Compared to normal rice it contains four times as much iron and twice as much selenium. It is also packed full of anthocyanins which are powerful antioxidants.

SUMMER VEGETABLE ROLLS

Ingredients for 6-8 people
Preparation time 1 hour 48-49 minutes
(45 minutes preparation + 1 hour resting + 3-4 minutes cooking)

4 sheets filo pastry or brik dough
1 3/4 oz. (50 g) carrot
2 3/4 oz. (80 g) yellow and red pepper
3 1/2 oz. (100 g) courgette
1 3/4 oz. (50 g) celery
2 tbsp. (30 ml) extra-virgin olive oil
3/4 oz. (20 g) butter
vegetable oil
salt and pepper

Preparation

Clean and wash all the vegetables.

Cut the vegetables into julienne and cook separately in a frying pan for 2-3 minutes making sure they remain crunchy. Lightly season with salt and pepper.

Lay out the sheets of filo pastry or brik dough on the worktop, brush with melted butter and place the vegetables on top.

Roll up the pastry and close the ends.

Fry in very hot oil, drain onto kitchen roll and cut into pieces.

PASTRY IN THIN LAYERS

Filo (or phyllo) pastry consists of paper-thin pastry sheets. The name drives from the Greek word "phullo" meaning leaf. Filo pastry is often used as a light casing for various roll recipes but also for other dishes when extremely thin layers of pastry are required. It has a neutral taste being made from only flour and water and is therefore suitable for savoury and sweet dishes. It is used throughout the world but its origin probably lies in Turkey, or at least in Central Asia, where this type of pastry is traditionally used to prepare baklava, a Middle Eastern dessert made with chopped nuts soaked in honey. Filo pastry dough is made from 40% water and 60% flour. Once the dough is formed into a block it is rolled out into very thin layers which are separated by cotton dishcloths to absorb any excess water and sprinkled with cornflour to prevent the pastry sheets from sticking together.

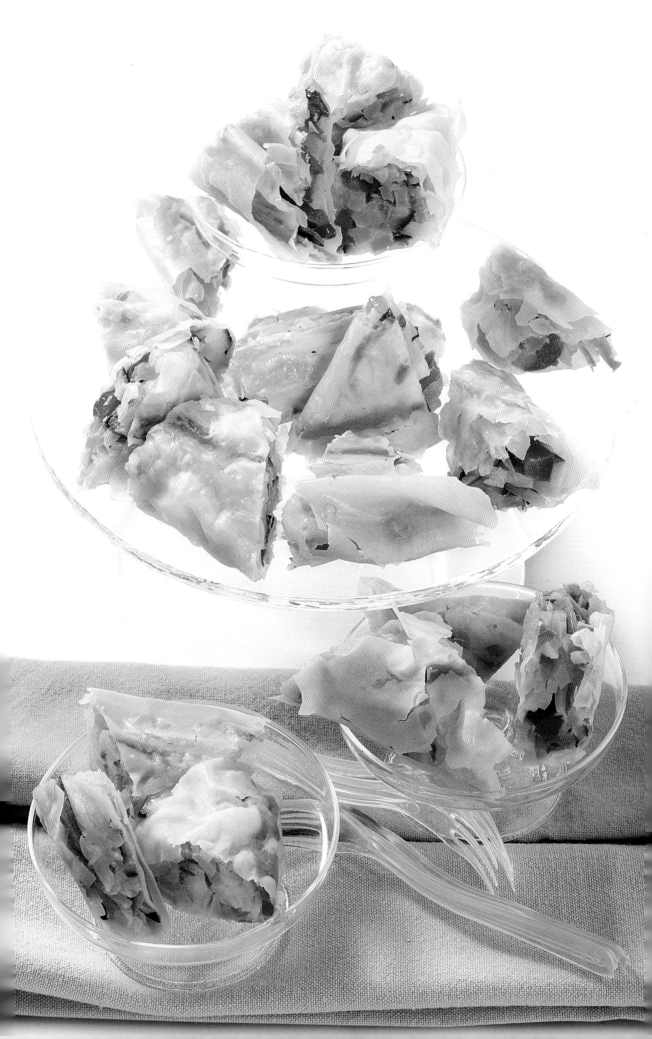

CARASAU FLATBREAD MILLE-FEUILLE WITH BURRATA CHEESE, TOMATOES AND BASIL-INFUSED OLIVE OIL

Ingredients for 4 people
Preparation time 1 hour 10 minutes (1 hour 10 minutes preparation)

1 carasau flatbread
10 1/2 oz. (300 g) tomatoes
4 tbsp. (60 ml) extra-virgin olive oil
3 1/2 oz. (100 g) burrata cheese
2 tsp. (10 g) sugar
1 garlic clove
1 bunch basil
oregano
salt

Preparation

Wash the tomatoes, make a small incision in the skin using the tip of a knife and place in boiling water for 30 seconds. Drain, place in ice-cold water to cool and peel. Cut each tomato into four, remove the seeds and place in a baking tray lined with greaseproof paper. Peel the garlic clove and cut into slices. Season the tomatoes with the garlic, a pinch of salt and pepper, the sugar, oregano and a dash of olive oil. Cook in the oven at 190-210°F (90-100°C) for approximately 1 hour.

Prepare the basil-infused oil. Wash the basil and blanch in boiling water for 30 seconds. Drain and leave to cool in ice-cold water. Blend with half of the extra-virgin olive oil.

Break the carasau flatbread into pieces, sprinkle with cold water (don't do this if you prefer crispy) and drizzle over some olive oil.

Build small mille-feuille cakes by alternating the carasau flatbread, tomatoes and burrata cheese.

Drizzle over the basil-infused olive oil and serve.

A SYMPHONY OF CRISP NOTES

Originally from the province of Nuoro before becoming popular throughout Sardinia, carasau flatbread (form the Sardinian verb "carasare" meaning to bake twice) is known in Italy as "music paper" thanks to its crispness which translates to music as it is eaten by itself or as an accompaniment to other savoury or sweet dishes. Carasau flatbread was most probably already being made at the time of Nuragic civilisation during the bronze age. This very thin flatbread, made using a dough consisting of water, durum wheat flour, yeast and salt, keeps for very long time. Over the years this characteristic has made it the ideal bread for the Sardinian agricultural and pastoral lifestyle.

FRIED MOZZARELLA SANDWICHES

Ingredients for 4 people
Preparation time 30 minutes (25 minutes preparation + 5 minutes cooking)

4 slices sandwich loaf bread
4 1/2 oz. (125 g) mozzarella
5 1/2 oz. (150 g) breadcrumbs
2 eggs
milk
all-purpose flour
vegetable oil
salt

Preparation

Remove the crust from the slices of bread and cut them into four.

Slice the mozzarella.

Place a piece of mozzarella between two slices of bread. Wet the edges of the bread with milk and press to seal the edges together.

Beat the eggs and season with a pinch of salt. Coat the small mozzarella sandwiches in flour, the beaten egg and then breadcrumbs.

Repeat this operation to ensure a more resistant coating.

Fry the mozzarella sandwiches in lots of hot oil for approximately 5 minutes.

Drain on to kitchen roll and serve while still hot so the mozzarella remains stringy.

A SNACK FROM CAMPANIA

Fried mozzarella sandwiches are a speciality of Campania but also popular in Lazio. This is another recipe created to recycle leftovers, in this case mozzarella which is no longer fresh, to produce a tasty snack. Necessity is the mother of invention and Italian cooking is full of recipes that use leftovers and products that can no longer be eaten on their own. This crispy and tasty appetiser, made with sandwich loaf bread and a mozzarella filling, is coated in flour, eggs and breadcrumbs and then fried. Anchovies or ham can be added to the filling to create an even tastier dish. Sandwiches have never tasted so good...

MINI SAVOURY PEANUT SBRISOLONA TARTS

Ingredients for 6-8 people
Preparation time 35 minutes (20 minutes preparation + 15 minutes cooking)

3 1/2 oz. (100 g) all-purpose flour
1 oz. (25 g) maize flour
1 oz. (25 g) dextrose
1 3/4 oz. (50 g) Parmigiano Reggiano cheese, grated
2 3/4 oz. (75 g) butter
3 oz. (2 1/2 + 1/2) 90 g (75 + 15) peanuts
1 egg yolk
salt

Preparation

Coarsely chop the peanuts. We will use 2 1/2 oz. (75 g) for the dough and 1/2 oz. (15 g) for final decoration.

Mix all the ingredients together (except for the egg yolk) to form a grainy heterogeneous dough in exactly the same way as if making a classic sbrisolona tart. Add the egg yolk and continue mixing.

Place the dough in small tartlet moulds, pressing down slightly, and sprinkle over a pinch of salt.

Sprinkle some peanuts on top and bake in the oven at 350°F (180°C) until golden brown (approximately 15 minutes).

PULSES, NOT DRIED FRUIT

Peanuts, also known colloquially in Italian as "spagnoletta" or "nocciolina americana", are pulses rather than dried fruit as many people wrongly believe. They can be toasted and eaten whole or ground into a paste. Peanut butter, ubiquitous in the United States of America, is nothing more than peanut paste mixed with vegetable oil, salt and sugar. Peanuts can also be transformed into a highly prized cooking oil. Only olive oil has a higher smoke point. The most common use for toasted and salted peanuts is as a tasty snack to go with an aperitif. Peanuts can also be toasted, coated in sugar and caramelised. Health benefits too. Peanuts are rich in protein, antioxidants, polyphenols and coenzyme Q10. In the Disney cartoon not for nothing is Goofy transformed into his superhero alter ego, Super Goof by eating peanuts.

PEPPERS STUFFED WITH FRESH CAPRINO GOAT'S CHEESE

Ingredients for 4 people
Preparation time 1 hour 50 minutes
(30 minutes preparation + 20 minutes cooking + 1 hour resting)

1 red pepper
1 yellow pepper
10 1/2 oz. (300 g) fresh caprino goat's cheese
valerian
extra-virgin olive oil
salt and pepper

Preparation

Pre-heat the oven to 375°F (190°C). Wash the peppers and roast them for approximately 20 minutes. Make sure they remain quite firm to the touch. Peel and clean the peppers then cut in half lengthways.

Beat the goat's cheese with a spoon to soften it.

Place the peppers on the worktop and season with salt and pepper. Use a piping bag to pipe a strip of goat's cheese along the length of each pepper half.

Using a sheet of cling film wrap the peppers around the cheese and place in the fridge for an hour to harden.

Cut the peppers into wheels with a sharp knife and serve with the valerian dressed with a dash of olive oil.

HALLUCINOGENIC, BUT ONLY FOR CATS

Valerian, field salad and lamb's lettuce are just some of the names given to the edible leaf vegetable with the scientific name Valerianella locusta. Even though it belongs to the family Valerianaceae, it is very different to Valeriana officinalis. The latter – also known in Italy as "common valerian" or "cats' grass" because it has an hallucinogenic effect on cats to which they are extremely attracted – is a sedative and tranquilliser causing drowsiness. It is widely used in phytotherapy to reduce anxiety, lower blood pressure and induce hypnosis.

POTATO BLINIS
WITH CREAMED CAPRINO GOAT'S CHEESE AND CAVIAR

Ingredients for 8 people
Preparation time 1 hour 12 minutes (40 minutes preparation + 30 minutes resting + 2 minutes cooking each)

7 oz. (200 g) potato
6 1/2 tbsp. (100 ml) milk
3/4 oz. (20 g) all-purpose flour
1 egg
salt and pepper
3/4 oz. (20 g) butter
1 lemon

1 3/4 oz. (50 g) red onion
5 tbsp. (75 ml) white wine vinegar
2 tsp. (10 g) sugar
5 1/2 oz. (150 g) caprino goat's
  cheese cream
caviar

Preparation

Chop the onion and heat in a pan with the vinegar and sugar. When the mixture starts to boil, remove from the heat and pour off the liquid.

Peel the potatoes and cook in a large pan of boiling salted water. Weigh out 3 1/2 oz. (100 g) of potato.

Mash the potato in a bowl and add the flour, egg and milk. Season with salt and pepper. Mix the ingredients to obtain a dense batter.

Leave to rest for approximately 30 minutes. Grease a non-stick frying with butter and cook the blinis by pouring 1 tablespoon of batter at a time into the pan. Cook and turn over to finish cooking on the other side. Repeat until you have used all the batter.

The blinis should be approximately 1/4 inch (1/2 cm) thick.

Beat the goat's cheese with a spoon to soften it. If necessary add a drop of cream.

Peel the lemon making sure you remove all the pith and cut into segments.

Spread some goat's cheese on each blini using a piping bag. Garnish with caviar, a piece of onion and a lemon segment.

FRESH, TASTY AND LIGHT PLEASURE

In Italian the word "caprino" means any number of a variety of cream, soft and semi-soft cheeses made from goat's milk and a greater or lesser percentage of cow's milk. These cheeses are produced throughout Italy from Piedmont to Sicily. Caprino is fresh, tasty and light. It can be used to add that something extra to a salad, or a plate of grilled vegetables or served as an accompaniment to an aperitif. Soft goat's cheese is also delicious spread on a crisp slice of bread with a dash of olive oil and a pinch of pepper.

CACIOCAVALLO CHEESE MUFFINS

Ingredients for approximately 15 small muffins
Preparation time 22 minutes (10 minutes preparation + 12 minutes cooking)

2 eggs
4 tsp. (20 ml) extra-virgin olive oil
4 3/4 tbsp. (70 ml) milk
3/4 oz. (20 g) Parmigiano Reggiano cheese, grated
4 3/4 oz. (135 g) all-purpose flour
2 tsp. (10 g) baking powder
3 1/2 oz. (100 g) caciocavallo cheese
nutmeg
salt and pepper

Preparation

Dice the caciocavallo.

Beat the eggs in a bowl with the oil and milk, grated Parmigiano Reggiano, salt, pepper and a pinch of nutmeg.

Add the flour mixed with the baking powder and then the diced cheese.

Mix all the ingredients without overdoing it.

Pour the mixture into paper muffin moulds so they are three quarters full and bake in the oven at 350°F (180°C) for approximately 12 minutes.

RUSTIC YET DELICIOUS

Muffins are small sweet cakes which originated in the United States where, along with Great Britain, they are widely consumed. Excellent for breakfast or afternoon tea, muffins have a moist, crumbly texture and look very much like cupcakes. They can be made from various types of dough enhanced by chocolate drops, blueberries, diced banana, almonds, walnuts or coconut to name just a few variations. The first muffins were made at the start of the eighteenth century as a peasant dish using dough made from stale bread, biscuit dough off-cuts and boiled potatoes. Today's muffins are tasty enough to satisfy even the most refined palate. Over the years savoury versions have become increasingly popular with cheese, vegetables and meat being added to the dough. Bite-size savoury muffins are the ideal accompaniment to an aperitif. A tasty snack with humble origins.

MINI VEGETABLE STRUDELS

Ingredients for 12 mini strudels
Preparation time 1 hour 15 minutes (1 hour preparation + 15 minutes cooking)

7 oz. (200 g) puff pastry
3 1/2 oz. (100 g) courgette
3 1/2 oz. (100 g) carrot
1 3/4 oz. (50 g) peas
3 1/2 oz. (100 g) peppers
1/2 leek
1/2 medium-sized aubergine
3 1/2 tbsp. (50 ml) extra-virgin olive oil
1 garlic clove
1 egg
sesame seeds, sunflower seeds, flaxseeds, etc.
salt and pepper

Preparation

Dice the courgette and sauté in a frying pan with the garlic and olive oil. Do the same with the aubergine, peppers and carrot. Blanch the peas for a couple of minutes in boiling salted water.

Roll out the pastry into a rectangle with a thickness of 1/16 inch (2 mm) and brush the edges with egg wash.

Layer the vegetable filling on the dough, roll up the pastry and place on a baking tray lined with greaseproof paper.

Make a few small cuts in the surface of the strudel to allow the steam to escape during cooking. Brush with the remaining egg wash and garnish with sesame seeds, sunflower seeds, flaxseeds, etc.

Bake in the oven at 350°F (180°C) for approximately 15 minutes.

When cooked, leave the strudel to cool and cut into slices.

THE SWEET VARIANT

As well as tasty savory strudels, thinly sliced and served as part of a buffet meal or as an accompaniment to an aperitif, there are also sweet strudels. The most famous of all is undoubtedly apple strudel. Originally from Turkey, where the remarkably similar baklava is still made today, apple strudel is now a culinary speciality of Trentino and South Tyrol, regions famous for their orchards producing high-quality apples. The traditional apple strudel recipe uses pippin apples with raisins, pine nuts and cinnamon. Alternatively sweeter Golden Delicious apples can be used.

FRIED MINI PIZZAS

Ingredients for 4-6 people
Preparation time 1 hour 55 minutes
(20 minutes preparation + 1 hour 30 minutes proving + 5 minutes cooking)

FOR THE DOUGH
9 oz. (250 g) pizza flour
1/2 cup water
2 tbsp. (10 g) fresh yeast
1 tsp. (5 g) salt
vegetable oil

FOR THE TOPPING
9 oz. (250 g) cherry tomatoes
1 garlic clove
1 tbsp. (15 ml) extra-virgin olive oil
salt and pepper
basil

Preparation

Dissolve the yeast in half a cup of water at room temperature or alternatively break it up over the flour. Mix the flour with the water and yeast. Dissolve the salt in 3 1/2 tbsp (50 ml) of water and add. Mix into a dough.

Cover with a dishcloth and leave to proof in a warm place until the dough has doubled in size (approximately one hour).

Divide the dough into pieces (approximately 1/2 oz., 10-20 g each). Form the pieces into balls and leave to proof again until they have doubled in size (approximately half an hour).

In the meantime wash the cherry tomatoes and cut them in half. Peel the garlic. Heat the whole glove of garlic in a pan with olive oil. Add the cherry tomatoes, season with salt and pepper and cook for no more than a few minutes. Remove the garlic and keep to one side.

Sprinkle some flour on a worktop and use your hands to flatten the balls of dough. Fry the mini pizzas a few at a time in a frying pan with lots of very hot oil.

When slightly brown drain using a skimmer and season with salt. Wash and dry the basil. Garnish the mini pizzas with the cherry tomatoes and basil.

THE POOR SISTER OF OVEN-BAKED PIZZA

Originally from Campania, fried pizza is the "poor sister of oven-baked pizza". This fried street food became popular immediately after the Second World War and is an excellent way of eating pizza topped with only tomato sauce and basil. Other toppings include ricotta cheese, provola cheese, mozzarella cheese, scarole, sausage and a variety of cold cuts.

FRIED POLENTA

Ingredients for 4 people
Preparation time 1 hour 4-5 minutes (1 hour preparation + 4-5 minutes cooking)

2 cups (500 ml) water
4 1/2 oz. (125 g) maize flour
olive oil for frying
salt

Preparation

Prepare the polenta by sprinkling the maize four into boiling salted water. If possible use a copper pan.

Cook the polenta for approximately 1/2 hour stirring frequently with a wooden spoon.

Pour the cooked polenta into a greased baking tray to create a thickness of approximately one centimeter. Leave to cool. When cool cut the polenta into shapes using a pastry cutter or simply cut into finger-sized pieces.

Heat the oil to a high temperature in a frying pan. Put the polenta pieces in the pan. Fry for 4-5 minutes until a nice golden crust has formed on the outside of the polenta pieces. Remove the polenta using a perforated spoon and place on kitchen roll to dry. Season with salt and serve immediately.

THE MANY TASTES OF POLENTA

Made from yellow or white maize flour depending on local tradition, polenta was the staple peasant food for whole generations in the regions of Northern Italy. It was eaten freshly cooked at lunchtime, kept for the evening meal, when it was cut into slices and toasted over an open fire or on the stove, and even served the following morning at breakfast with milk. Often polenta was the only foodstuff available whereas today it is served as an accompaniment to tasty and flavourful dishes. Traditionally it is served with meat, fish or cheese sauces but is also excellent with mushrooms, truffles and beans. The most famous regional uses in Italy include polenta and salted dried cod from Vicenza, polenta and snails from Ascoli Piceno, polenta bake from Friuli made with meat sauce and cheese, buckwheat polenta cooked in cream from the Valtellina, and polenta with fontina cheese, anchovies and tomatoes from Monferrato.

AUBERGINE BALLS

Ingredients for 6 people
Preparation time 45-55 minutes
(15 minutes preparation + 30-40 + 3 minutes cooking)

1 aubergine (approx. 10 1/2 oz / 300 g)
3-4 mint leaves
3 1/2 oz. (100 g) breadcrumbs
1 1/2 oz. (40 g) Parmigiano Reggiano cheese, grated
vegetable oil
salt

Preparation

Wash and dry the aubergine. Wrap the aubergine in tin foil and cook in the oven at 350°F (180°C) for approximately 30-40 minutes until the aubergine is very soft.

Leave to cool, remove the skin and wring out the remaining water. Dice the aubergine. Add the washed dried and chopped mint. Season with salt then add the Parmigiano Reggiano and enough breadcrumbs to obtain a mixture with medium consistency.

Mould the mixture into small balls, coat in the remaining breadcrumbs and fry in very hot oil.

Drain on kitchen roll and serve.

THE AROMA OF FRESHNESS

The word mint is rooted in the Greek word minthe, personified in Greek mythology as Minthe, a nymph who was the object of Pluto's lust and was transformed into a mint plant. Mint, a perennial flowering plant with a spicy and pungent flavour, belongs to the Labiatae family. Already known at the time of the ancient Egyptians and ancient Romans for its digestive, antiseptic and antispasmodic properties, today mint is grown in Europe, Asia and Africa. Many different varieties are cultivated but the most well-known one is peppermint which originated in the United Kingdom. Its refreshing taste and intense fragrance make it popular in the preparation of confectionary and chewing gum. In the kitchen the strong flavour of mint makes it ideal for use with meats that also have an intense flavour such as lamb, mutton and duck. The flavour is also fresh meaning mint can be used to enhance summer vegetables such as courgettes, tomatoes, aubergines and cucumbers as well as fruit salad and sweet coulis. Mint is also used to aromatise tea and cocktails.

CHEESE PASTRY PUFFS

Ingredients for 8 people
Preparation time 32 minutes (20 minutes preparation + 12 minutes cooking)

5 1/2 oz. (150 g) puff pastry
3/4 oz. (20 g) butter
1 oz. (25 g) flour
2/3 cup (150 ml) milk
3 1/2 oz. (100 g) fontina (or similar semi-hard cheese)
salt and pepper

Preparation

Melt the butter in a pan, add the flour and cook for a couple of minutes but do not brown.

Add the milk, bring to the boil, cook for one or two minutes and season with salt. Leave to cool completely.

Cut the cheese into small cubes and add to the béchamel sauce.

Roll out the puff pastry to a thickness of approximately 1/16 inch (2 mm). Use a fork to prick holes in the dough and then line small individual moulds with the pastry.

Add the filling, season with a pinch of pepper and bake in the oven at 350°F (180°C) for approximately 12 minutes.

MELTING PLEASURE

Fontina has Protected Origin Designation status and was first made in the Italian Alpine Aosta Valley region nine hundred years ago. This full-fat cheese is either aged or medium-aged. It is a semi-soft cheese with a straw yellow colour. It is aromatic, pliable and buttery with small to medium-sized, unevenly distributed holes. The orange-brown washed rind is soft and thin. The distinctive cooking feature of fontina is that it melts at 60°C. For this reason it is the main ingredient in cheese fondue and all those recipes involving cheese which melts easily. It is therefore used to make béchamel and many other types of sauces.

PUGLIA BREAD AND SCAMORZA CHEESE KEBABS

Ingredients for 6 kebabs
Preparation time 23 minutes (20 minutes preparation + 3 minutes cooking)

2 oz. (60 g) scamorza cheese
2 thick slices Puglia bread
1 3/4 oz. (50 g) all-purpose flour
1 egg
3 1/2 oz. (100 g) breadcrumbs
vegetable oil
salt

Preparation

Cut the bread and cheese into similar-size chunks and thread alternately onto wooden or bamboo skewers

Beat the egg in a bowl with a pinch of salt.

Coat the kebabs in flour, the beaten egg and the breadcrumbs making sure the latter stick properly.

Fry the kebabs in very hot oil, drain onto kitchen roll and serve.

PRINCE OF SOUTHERN ITALIAN CHEESES

Usually made from cow's milk (but in Campania there is a variant made with buffalo milk), scamorza is a stretched curd cheese. It seems the name derives from the verb "scamozzare" which means to "eliminate a part": This may refer to the technique used by the cheese maker to split the curd to produce the distinctive pear-like shape. This process is also known as strangling because it involves string being tied round the upper part of the cheese. The ivory-coloured rind of scamorza is smooth, pliable and thin whereas the cheese itself is light yellow in colour, semi-soft, mild and without holes. Scamorza can be left to mature in which case the rind is golden brown and the cheese is straw yellow in colour and stronger. Widely consumed in Campania, Abruzzo, Molise and Puglia, scamorza is eaten on its own and also used as an ingredient in cooking. The origins of this cheese go back a long way. Neapolitan nativity scenes from the seventeenth century depict shepherds holding scamorza.

FENNEL CRACKERS

Ingredients for 6 people
Preparation time 1 hour 30 minutes
(45 minutes preparation + 15 minutes resting + 30 minutes cooking)

9 oz. (250 g) all-purpose flour
3 1/2 tbsp. (50 ml) dry white wine
4 tbsp. (60 ml) extra-virgin olive oil
2 tbsp. (30 ml) water
1 tbsp. (6 g) fennel seeds
1 tsp. (5 g) salt

Preparation

Mix the flour with the white wine, oil, salt and enough water to obtain a smooth and pliable dough. Add the fennel seeds towards the end of the mixing process.

Wrap the dough in cling film and leave to rest for at least 15 minutes.

Divide the dough into strips with a section of approximately one centimeter. Trim the strips to approximately 8 centimeters in length and mould them into small donuts by joining together the ends of the dough.

Put them into a pan with lots of boiling salted water. Drain using a perforated spoon as soon as they come to the surface.

Dry using a dishcloth and place on a lightly oiled baking tray.

Bake in the oven at 350°F (180°C) for approximately 20 minutes until golden brown.

AN APPETISING SNACK

Taralli crackers originated in puglia but are also a traditional food of Campania, Calabria and Sicily. They are made by cooking rings of unleavened dough in boiling water which are then baked in the oven. The dough usually consists of water, flour, wine, olive oil and salt but can vary depending on the place of origin. A whole range of tasty ingredients can be added to enhance the flavour. There are sweet versions but the savoury variety is an excellent snack to be eaten between meals or to accompany an aperitif. Originally peasant and street food, first made to use off-cuts of leavened dough, today taralli crackers are an ideal accompaniment to a cocktail or glass of wine.

MIXED FRIED VEGETABLES

Ingredients for 6-8 people
Preparation time 35 minutes (30 minutes preparation + 5 minutes cooking)

3 1/2 oz. (100 g) courgette
3 1/2 oz. (100 g) peppers
3 1/2 oz. (100 g) fennel
3 1/2 oz. (100 g) asparagus
1 artichoke
1 3/4 oz. (50 g) all-purpose flour
1 1/2 oz. (40 g) corn flour
6 3/4 tbsp. (100 ml) ice-cold sparkling water
vegetable oil
salt

Preparation

Wash and clean all the vegetables and cut into chip-size pieces.

Heat lots of oil in a large frying pan.

In the meantime prepare the batter by mixing the flour, corn flour, a pinch of salt and ice-cold water.

Coat the vegetable sticks in batter and fry in the very hot oil.

Drain using a perforated spoon and leave to dry on kitchen roll.

Season with salt and serve the vegetables while still very hot.

TRICKS FOR BEAUTIFUL BATTER

Tempura is a Japanese dish of vegetables and seafood (usually prawns and squid) that have been battered and deep fried. The dish may have been imported into Japan by Portuguese Jesuits. The name "tempura" comes form the Latin "quattro tempora" which were the four periods of the year when monks gave up meat. There are three tricks for making perfect batter. First of all the water must be ice-cold and, if possible, also fizzy. A good tip is to add some ice cubes to prevent the temperature from rising. Secondly, do not mix the flour and water too much making sure you leave lumps in the mixture. The third trick is oil temperature. The ingredients should be deep fried, a few pieces at a time, in oil at a temperature of 180°C (350°F). This simple tips should help you make tempura that is crispy without being too greasy.

TOMME CHEESE BISCUITS

Ingredients for 6-8 portions
Preparation time 1 hour 28-29 minutes
(15 minutes preparation + 1 hour resting + 13-14 minutes cooking)

FOR THE SHORT CRUST PASTRY
3 1/2 oz. (100 g) all-purpose flour
1 3/4 oz. (50 g) butter
1-1 1/2 tbsp. (15-20 ml) water
1/2 tsp. (2 g) salt

FOR THE TOMME CHEESE
9 oz. (250 g) fresh tomme cheese
1 hot chilli pepper
extra-virgin olive oil

Preparation

For the short crust pastry cut the butter into small pieces and mix with the flour to form a grainy heterogeneous dough.

Add the salt and cold water and mix to obtain a uniform dough without over-kneading.

Wrap the dough in cling film and leave to stand in the fridge for at least an hour.

Roll out the pastry to a thickness of approximately 1/16 inch (2 mm). Use a fork to prick holes in the dough. Cut the dough into circles using a small pastry cutter.

Place the pastry circles in a baking tray lined with greaseproof paper and bake in the oven at 390°F (180°C) for approximately 13-14 minutes.

Leave to cool. Place some cheese on each biscuit. Garnish with the hot chilli pepper and a drizzle of olive oil.

SMALL TOMME CHEESE FROM PIEDMONT

Small tomme is a traditional cheese of Piedmont. There are more than ten official variants. It is a full-fat or half-fat cheese made from a mixture of cow's milk and sheep's and/or goat's milk. Originally it was made only from goat's milk. It is available as a young cheese in which case it is soft, buttery, moist and white. The flavour is mild with a pleasant aroma, like fresh milk, but with a slightly sour scent. It is also available as a mature cheese and in this case it is covered in a thin rind and the cheese is more compact. The colour is straw yellow and the flavour is fuller. Tomme produces an intense and persistent aroma when melted in the oven, in a pan, on a griddle or on a soapstone. It is a very simple yet tasty cheese and is used in dozens of Italian cooking recipes. As well as adding flavour to numerous recipes, Tomme cheese is delicious on its own or with a dash of extra-virgin olive oil and aromatic herbs.

ONION AND BLACK OLIVE SAVOURY TART

Ingredients for 12 portions
Preparation time 2 hours 20 minutes
(1 hour preparation + 1 hour resting + 20 minutes cooking)

FOR THE SHORT CRUST PASTRY
7 oz. (200 g) all-purpose flour
3 1/2 oz. (100 g) butter
1 3/4-2 tbsp. (25-30 ml) water
1/4 tsp. (4 g) salt

FOR THE FILLING
3/4 + 1 1/2 oz. (20 + 40 g) butter

3 1/2 tsp. (18 g) all-purpose flour
1 cup (250 ml) milk
4 1/4 oz. (120 g) mild provolone cheese
12 1/2 oz. (350 g) onion
1 oz. (30 g) pitted black olives
1 egg yolk
nutmeg
salt and pepper

Preparation

For the short crust pastry cut the butter into small pieces and mix with the flour to form a "sandy" heterogeneous dough.

Add the salt and cold water and mix to obtain a uniform dough without over-kneading.

Wrap the dough in cling film and leave to stand in the fridge for at least an hour.

In the meantime melt 3/4 oz. (20 g) of butter in a small pan. Add the flour, cook for one minute, add the milk, a pinch of salt, pepper and nutmeg and bring to the boil. Leave to cool and add the egg.

Melt the remaining 1 1/2 oz. (40 g) of butter. Finely slice the onions, add to the butter and sweat over a low heat for approximately 10 minutes without browning. Season with salt and pepper.

Add the onions to the béchamel sauce. Grate the provolone and add.

Roll out the short crust pastry to a thickness of approximately 1/16 inch (2 mm). Line a quiche tin with greaseproof paper and then the pastry. Use a fork to prick holes in the dough and then pour in the onion mixture.

Sprinkle the black olives over the top and bake in the oven at 350°F (180°C) for approximately 20 minutes.

Remove from the oven, leave to cool and cut into squares.

A TASTY PEACE OFFERING

Olive trees, producers of an oily, fleshy fruit with a meaty consistency, were cultivated for the first time on the island of Crete between 5000 and 3000 BC before spreading to Greece, Palestine and Asia Minor. Not only is it an important plant for the human diet, but has also been a symbol of peace since ancient times.

SPINACH RICE CAKES

Ingredients for 6-8 people
Preparation time 1 hour (20 minutes preparation + 40 minutes cooking)

9 oz. (250 g) Roma rice
1.1 lb (500 g) fresh spinach
2 cups (500 ml) vegetable stock (or water)
3 1/2 oz. (100 g) Parmigiano Reggiano cheese, grated
1 3/4 oz. (50 g) onion
3/4 oz. (20 g) butter
2 eggs
1 bay leaf
breadcrumbs
pepper

Preparation

Wash the spinach thoroughly, drain and coarsely chop.

Finely chop the onion, melt half the butter in a pan and sweat the onion with the bay leaf. Remove the bay leaf.

Add the rice and toast stirring continuously. Add the spinach, cook for a few seconds and add the vegetable stock (or water).

Lightly season with salt and cook for approximately 10 minutes adding more stock or water if necessary. The final consistency should be fairly fluid.

Remove from the heat and leave to cool then add the eggs and half the grated Parmigiano Reggiano.

Grease some small moulds with the remaining butter and sprinkle over some breadcrumbs.

Pour the rice into the moulds, sprinkle some breadcrumbs over the top and bake in the oven at 340°F (170°C) for approximately half an hour.

Leave to cool before removing the rice cakes from the moulds and serve at room temperature.

IDEAL FOR RISOTTOS

First produced in 1931, Roma rice like other rice varieties such as Arborio, Carnaroli, Argo and Baldo is a short-grain rice. It has a rounded grain which releases lots of starch during cooking. It is this high percentage of starch which makes it ideal for making smooth, creamy risottos.

DOUBLE-COOKED QUAIL EGGS

Ingredients for 4 people
Preparation time 18 minutes and 30 seconds
(15 minutes preparation + 3 minutes and 30 seconds cooking)

8 quail eggs
1 egg
3 1/2 oz. (100 g) breadcrumbs
all-purpose flour
vegetable oil
salt

Preparation

Beat the egg in a bowl with a pinch of salt.

Put the quail eggs in a pan, cover with water and bring to the boil.

Boil for 2 and a half minutes.

Drain the quail eggs and place in cold water to stop the cooking process and facilitate shelling.

Shell the quail eggs then coat in flour, beaten egg and breadcrumbs and then again in the egg and breadcrumbs.

Fry the eggs in a frying pan with very hot oil.

Fry for one minute until golden brown, drain using a perforated spoon and leave to dry on kitchen roll.

Season to taste with salt and serve.

A SMALL TREASURE CHEST OF NUTRIENTS

Quail eggs are used in exactly the same way as chicken eggs but they are much more delicate and do not contain bad LDL cholesterol. They are rich in many nutrients including phosphorous, calcium, potassium, protein and vitamins. Quail eggs are produced by birds with a brown head which are farmed in exactly the same way as chickens. The eggs are smaller than those from chickens and their shells have black, grey and brown spots rather than a uniform colour. The eggs weigh approximately 3/4 oz to 1 oz (20-30 g) each with the shell and approximately 1/3 oz. (9 g) when shelled which is a about a fifth of a chicken egg. They are not widely consumed in Italy, unlike some other countries around the world such as Japan, for example, where quail eggs are eaten freshly hatched and raw.

FISH DELIGHTS

Brik stuffed with asparagus and king prawns, stuffed sardine lollipops, salmon and sole pinwheels, curried bream croquettes, swordfish roulades, terrine of greater amberjack, prawns and Savoy cabbage, purée of salted dried cod with sautéed purple potatoes. Just hearing these names is enough to wet the appetite. They also show that appetizers are an elegant and tempting way of serving fish. Unlike with main courses you can be more adventurous when preparing fish appetizers. People are far more prepared to try something new when they only have to eat one or two mouthfuls. Don't be afraid to explore new and unusual combinations. Surprise yourself with a blend of unexpected flavours.

Fish is often overlooked as a day-to-day ingredient even though it is one of the most nutritious foods available to us. It is low in fat and the best natural source of essential Omega 3 fatty acids which are offer protection against a whole series of illnesses. Fish is also packed with protein and mineral salts such as calcium and phosphorous. Recent research has also shown that shellfish, such as scampi and prawns, long considered as being high in cholesterol, is much healthier than previously thought.

The lightest fish appetizers are those prepared in the simplest way both in terms of the ingredients used and the cooking method involved. Octopus salad cones, scallops with pumpkin and orange, prawns in hazelnut crust, grilled salmon with red pepper coulis, swordfish and lime kebabs and grilled squid salad with thyme dressing are all full of flavour but in reality very simple dishes. Some of the recipes, such as sea bass carpaccio, sea bass and salmon tartare and anchovies marinated in pink pepper on toast, use raw fish. These dishes allow us to appreciate fully the consistency, flavour and aroma of fish and to benefit as much as possible from its nutritive power without any interference from cooking or elaborate preparation.

Some of the fish recipes are deliberately more complex to enhance the flavour of the sea in symphony with, or opposition to, other ingredients. King prawn cocktail with marinated cherry tomatoes and guacamole combines freshness with rich and intense flavours. The flavours in the meat used to make mussel kebabs with courgette and smoked bacon exalt the flavour of the molluscs. Couscous salad with chickpeas, mussels, clams and prawns combines North African tradition with Italian legume flavours using fish to bridge the gap between the southern and northern shorelines of the Mediterranean Sea.

FRIED ANCHOVIES

Ingredients for 4 people
Preparation time 22 minutes (20 minutes preparation + 2 minutes cooking)

7 oz. (200 g) anchovies
3 1/2 oz. (100 g) semolina
vegetable oil
salt

Preparation

Clean the anchovies by removing the head, guts and fishbone. Butterfly the anchovies, rinse and dry. Coat in the semolina.

Fry the anchovies in lots of very hot oil, drain using a skimmer, leave to dry on kitchen roll and season with salt.

Serve in chip cones.

A SMALL BUT TASTY FISH

The anchovy (scientific name Engraulis encrasicolus) is fish variety of the Engraulidae family. Anchovies are found in the Eastern Atlantic Ocean, Sea of Azov, Black Sea and Mediterranean Sea. They have long bodies with scales and small head and range in length from from 4 3/4 inches to 7 3/4 inches (12-20 cm). They are green with blue reflections due to the silver-coloured longitudinal stripe that runs from the base of the caudal fin They also have a distinctive crossways line which is usually brown but also a beautiful electric blue in the most esteemed varieties. Anchovy flesh is extremely tasty and can be eaten cooked in the oven or fried (as in the case of our recipe). Anchovies can also be eaten raw if marinated or preserved in salt. Desalted anchovies can be ground using a pestle and mortar or food processor to make anchovy paste similar to the garum prepared in ancient times. The latter was a delicacy used as a condiment in ancient Roman cooking. It was made by fermenting fish intestines and salted fish in the sun with the addition of strong-flavoured aromatic herbs such as dill, coriander, fennel, celery, mint, pepper, saffron and oregano.

PURÉE OF SALTED DRIED COD
WITH SAUTÉED PURPLE POTATOES

Ingredients for 4 people
Preparation time 1 hour (30 minutes preparation + 30 minutes cooking)

1 3/4 oz. (50 g) onion
10 1/2 oz. (300 g) soaked salted dried cod
1 garlic clove
1 cup (250 ml) milk
6 3/4 tbsp. (100 ml) extra-virgin olive oil
7 oz. (200 g) purple potatoes
vegetable oil
1 sprig thyme
salt and pepper

Preparation

Pour some of the olive oil into a pan, add the diced onion, skinless salted dried cod cut into small pieces, garlic clove and the sprig of thyme.

Cover with milk, season with salt and pepper, bring to the boil and allow to simmer for approximately 30 minutes.

In the meantime prepare the sautéed potatoes: peel the potatoes, wash then and cut into thin slices using a mandolin. Rinse under running water, drain thoroughly, dry with a dishcloth and fry in very hot oil for approximately 1 minute. Drain on kitchen roll. Season with salt.

When the salted dried cod is cooked and begins to break up, drain any excess milk, remove the garlic and thyme and purée using the remainder of the olive oil.

Serve the purée of salted dried cod warm in small portions accompanied by the sautéed purple potatoes.

A FISH FULL OF FLAVOUR

Salted dried cod is made using fish (scientific name Gadus Morhua) caught in the North Atlantic and preserved in salt. On the other hand stockfish is made from the same type of cod but the preservation method involves drying. Salting cod is a very old technique which seems to have been invented by Basque fishermen. Whale hunts led them to the North Atlantic where they discovered huge shoals of cod off the coast of Newfoundland. They decided to catch the cod and preserve the flesh with the same procedure already used for whale meat. Of course before use salted cod must be soaked for along time in cold water to remove the excess salt.

KING PRAWN COCKTAIL
WITH MARINATED CHERRY TOMATOES AND GUACAMOLE

Ingredients for 8 portions
Preparation time 1 hour 9-11 minutes
(30 minutes preparation + 30 minutes marinating + 9-11 minutes cooking)

20 cherry tomatoes
3/4 oz. (20 g) red onion
3 basil leaves
1 garlic clove
3 1/2 tbsp. (50 ml) extra-virgin olive oil
15 king prawns
1 chilli pepper

1 ripe avocado
1 lime
1 sheet filo pastry 8x12 inches (20x30 cm)
1 oz. (30 g) salted peanuts
1 egg white
salt and pepper

Preparation

Wash the cherry tomatoes and cut them into quarters. Put the tomatoes in a bowl. Wash, dry and chop the basil then add to the tomatoes. Peel the garlic and add the whole clove. Finely dice the onion and add. Season with salt, pepper and the extra-virgin olive oil. Leave to marinate for at least 30 minutes.

Place the sheet of filo pastry in a baking tray lined with greaseproof paper and brush with the beaten egg white. Sprinkle over the coarsely-chopped peanuts and bake in the oven at 350°F (180°C) for 8-10 minutes. Leave to cool and break up into uneven pieces.

In the meantime peel the avocado, remove the stone and mash using a fork to create a purée. Season with salt, pepper, lime juice and a teaspoon of olive oil.

Shell the king prawns, remove the guts and chop into small pieces. Sauté in a frying pan over a high heat with olive oil, salt and chilli pepper.

Put some cherry tomatoes in the cocktail glasses, add some sautéed king prawn and cover with guacamole.

Garnish with a piece of peanut biscuit and serve.

AN ONION WITH A SWEET CORE

Tropea red onion is the name given to this root vegetable imported into Italy by the Phoenicians and grown for over two thousand years in an area between Nicotera, in the province of Vibo Valentia, and Campo San Giovanni, in the province of Cosenza, and along the coast of the Tyrrhenian sea. The specific composition of the soil in these areas and the mild winter climate make Tropea red onions sweet rather than bitter. This vegetable, which owes its sweetness to the presence of sugars such as glucose, fructose and sucrose, is rich in vitamins C and E, iron, selenium, iodine, zinc and magnesium.

DIFFICULTY

POPPY SEED BISCUITS WITH SMOKED SALMON MOUSSE

Ingredients for approximately 15 biscuits
Preparation time 1 hour 47-48 minutes
(35 minutes preparation + 1 hour resting + 12-13 minutes cooking)

FOR THE BISCUITS
7 oz. (200 g) all-purpose flour
3 1/2 oz. (100 g) butter
1/2 oz. (15 g) poppy seeds
2 tbsp. (30 ml) water
1/4 tsp. (4 g) salt

FOR THE MOUSSE
1/2 oz. (15 g) smoked salmon
1 oz. (30 g) butter
salt and pepper

Preparation

Cut the butter into small pieces and mix with the flour to form a grainy heterogeneous dough.

Add the poppy seeds, salt and cold water and mix to obtain a uniform dough without over-kneading.

Mould the dough into a cylinder with diameter of approximately 1 1/2 inches (4 cm), wrap in cling film and leave to stand in the fridge for at least an hour.

Cut the dough into slices with thickness of approximately 1/6 inch (4 mm). Line a baking tray with greaseproof paper, put the biscuits in and bake in the oven at 390°F (180°C) for approximately 12-13 minutes.

Leave to cool.

In the meantime cut the butter into small pieces and blend with the salmon in a food processor. Season with salt and pepper.

Spread the salmon mousse on the biscuits and serve.

APHRODISIAC SEEDS

Poppy seeds are the edible oilseed of two poppy plants with the scientific names Papaver nigrum (black poppy) and Papaver setigerum (dwarf breadseed poppy). They are a rich source of nutrients especially manganese, calcium, linoleic acid (Omega 6) and vitamin E. They are usually used as a topping when baking both savoury and sweet dishes. They are popular in Trentino and South Tyrol where they are used to make the famous poppy seed strudel and citrus fruit tarts such as orange or lemon. Poppy seeds have been used in cooking since ancient times. The ancient Romans appreciated them not only for their taste but their supposed aphrodisiac powers. Before departing on their honeymoon, newlyweds were given a drink known as "cocetum" containing a large helping of poppy seeds.

SQUID STUFFED WITH BROAD BEANS AND OLIVES

Ingredients for 4-6 people
Preparation time 45 minutes (30 minutes preparation + 15 minutes cooking)

2 medium-sized squid
2 prawns
1/4 lemon (juice only)
1 3/4 oz. (50 g) fresh broad beans
1 3/4 oz. (50 g) carrot
1 3/4 oz. (10 g) pitted black olives
4 tsp. (20 ml) extra-virgin olive oil
1 egg white
salt and pepper

Preparation

Clean and wash the squid. Shell the prawns and remove the guts.

Remove the tentacles from the squid and cook in some water and the lemon juice. Coarsely chop the tentacles and finely chop the prawn tails.

Peel the carrot and dice finely (1/10 to 1/6 inch [3-4 mm]). Blanch the carrot and broad beans separately in boiling salted water and leave cool in ice-cold water. Remove the outer membrane from the broad beans.

Chop the olives.

Mix all the ingredients together with the egg white, season with salt and pepper and stuff the squid with the filling. Use a toothpick to seal the open end of the squid.

Lightly grease a roasting tin with olive oil and put the squid in the tin. Cook in the oven at 340°F (170°C) for approximately 15 minutes.

Slice and serve with a dash of olive oil.

THE INKPOT OF THE SEA

Squid, also known in Italian as "pesci calamaio" – literally inkpot fish – thanks to the very dark liquid, similar to ink, released as a mechanism for escape from predators, have been eaten since ancient times. The ancient Greeks were very fond of the tasty flesh. Then as now the way squid is used in the kitchen depends on their size. Smaller animals are more suited to being cooked whole, fried or added to seafood salads whereas larger ones are better stuffed or steamed. Squid are not just tasty they are also rich in nutrients including mineral salts, such as calcium and phosphorous, as well as vitamins A and B1. Moreover they are low in calories and cholesterol.

SCALLOPS WITH PUMPKIN AND ORANGE

Ingredients for 4 people
Preparation time 50 minutes (20 minutes preparation + 30 minutes cooking)

9 oz. (250 g) pumpkin
4 scallops
2 tsp. (10 ml) extra-virgin olive oil
1 orange
1/2 oz. (10 g) angel hair pasta
vegetable oil
salt and pepper

Preparation

Cook the pumpkin in the oven until very soft, peel, remove filaments and blend to produce a thick purée. Season with salt and pepper and keep warm.

Peel the orange making sure you also remove the pith. Cut the orange into segments and leave to one side. Squeeze the juice from the remains of the orange into a small pan.

Clean the scallops, dry them, season with salt and pepper and cook in a non-stick frying pan with a dash of olive oil or in a griddle pan for one minute.

Use a piping bag to form a finger of purée in the centre of each side plate, lay the scallop up against the pumpkin and garnish with orange segments and warm orange juice.

Garnish with a few strands of angel hair pasta fried in very hot oil.

THE MOLLUSC THAT GAVE BIRTH TO VENUS

Scallops (scientific name Pecten jacobaeus), also known as the pilgrim's scallop, are a marine bivalve mollusc with fan-shaped shell with a radiating, fluted pattern. The tasty flesh of scallops is highly prized in many cuisines but this animal also has an excellent reputation away from the kitchen. During the Middle Ages scallop shells were used by priests to pour water over those being christened. The scallop is the emblem of pilgrimage to Santiago de Compostela. It can also be seen in the coat of arms of Pope Benedict XVI. The scallop also plays a central role in Boticelli's painting The Birth of Venus which depicts the goddess Venus emerging from the sea in a scallop shell.

OCTOPUS SALAD CONES

Ingredients for 4 people
Preparation time 2 hours 35 minutes
(30 minutes preparation + 1 hour resting + 1 hour 5 minutes cooking)

FOR THE CONES
4 1/2 oz. (125 g) flour
4 tbsp. (60 ml) water
1 tbsp. (15 ml) extra-virgin olive oil
1 tsp. (4 g) baking powder
1/2 tsp. (3 g) salt

FOR THE OCTOPUS SALAD
10 1/2 oz. (300 g) octopus

1 onion
1 carrot
3 sticks celery
1 oz. (30 g) black olives
3 1/2 tbsp. (50 ml) extra-virgin olive oil
3/4 oz. (20 g) sundried tomatoes
1 lemon
1 tbsp. (2 g) parsley, chopped
salt and pepper

Preparation

Bring a pan of salted water to the boil. Peel the carrot and onion and wash the celery. Add the carrot, onion and 1 celery stick to the water when boiling.

Cook for 5 minutes and add the octopus. A good tip to keep the octopus tender is to dunk it quickly in the boiling water three times before actually adding it.

Cook for one hour or until soft. Insert a knife to check whether soft. When ready, switch OFF the heat, cover the pan and leave to cool for an hour.

Make the flour into a well on a pastry board. Add the water, baking powder, olive oil and salt. Mix the ingredients into a smooth and pliable dough.

Leave the dough to proof for at least an hour.

Roll out the dough to a thickness of approximately 1/32 to 1/16 inch (1-2 mm), cut into triangles and roll around the special metal cones. Use water to wet the edges so they stick together.

Fry in lots of very hot oil, drain, remove the metal cones and dry using kitchen roll.

Drain the octopus and cut into small pieces. Finely chop the remaining celery and sundried tomatoes and mix together with the olives and parsley. Make a dressing using the lemon juice, olive oil, salt and pepper. Drizzle over the remaining extra-virgin olive oil.

Fill the cones and serve.

THE MOST INTELLIGENT MOLLUSC IN THE SEA

The octopus is an invertebrate with supernatural powers. Their suction cups are able to taste the flavour of food, feel their way in a labyrinth and open tins and bottles. The octopus has innate acting skills: skin which changes colour to evade predators, tentacles which regenerate and and eyes with almost human-like qualities. What more do you want?

CURRIED BREAM CROQUETTES

Ingredients for 6 people
Preparation time 34-35 minutes
(30 minutes preparation + 4-5 minutes cooking)

7 oz. (200 g) skinless bream fillets
3 1/2 oz. (100 g) breadcrumbs
1 cup (250 ml) cream
1 egg white
3 1/2 oz. (100 g) all-purpose flour
2 eggs
7 oz. (200 g) thin noodles
vegetable oil
curry powder
salt

Preparation

Soak the breadcrumbs in the cream. Use a food processor to blend this mixture with the bream fillets, egg white, salt and curry powder.

Use a piping bag to form the mixture into shapes the size of a cork.

Break the thin noodles into small pieces. Coat the croquettes in flour, whisked eggs and then the noodles.

Heat the oil in a frying pan, fry the croquettes and drain on kitchen roll. Season with salt.

WRAP YOURSELF IN PLEASANT THREADS

Tagliolini is a traditional type of pasta from Piedmont and Molise. Individual pieces are flat ribbons with a width of 1/16 to 1/10 inch (2-3 mm), that is to say wider than capellini (angel hair) but narrower than tagliatelle. The thickness is less than 1/32 inch (1 mm) and the length similar to spaghetti. Tagliolini is made using a dough comprising flour, eggs and a pinch of salt. Its daintiness makes it ideal for light sauces such as plain butter or olive oil, tomato and basil, fish, vegetables and even stock. Known as "tajarin" in the Piedmont dialect, tagliolini was already being made in the Langhe and Monferrato during the fifteenth century. Today in these areas of Piedmont traditional sauces for tagliolini include shavings of black or white truffles, offal or game ragout, mushrooms and another local delicacy, Castelmagno cheese.

ANCHOVIES MARINATED IN PINK PEPPER ON TOAST

Ingredients for 4 people
Preparation time 98 hours
(30 minutes preparation + 96 hours freezing + 1 hour 30 minutes marinating)

12 anchovies
3 lemons
1 1/2 oz. (40 g) baby salad leaves
4 cherry tomatoes
2 tbsp. (30 ml) extra-virgin olive oil
1 baguette
pink pepper
salt

Preparation

Clean and fillet the anchovies Dry them well and lay them out carefully in a dish.

Freeze for at least 96 hours at 0°F (-18°C) to kill off any anisakis.

Season the anchovies with pink pepper and salt.

Cover the anchovies with the lemon juice keeping some in reserve to dress the baby salad leaves. Seal the dish with cling film and leave to marinate for an hour and a half. Drain off the liquid and dress the anchovies with a drizzle of olive oil.

Slice the baguette and sauté in a frying pan with a small amount of olive oil.

Place an anchovy fillet and a few pink peppercorns on each piece of bread.

Cut the cherry tomatoes into quarters and mix with the baby salad leaves. Dress the salad with salt, extra-virgin olive oil and the remaining lemon juice.

Serve the crostini accompanied by the salad.

THE MILDEST PART OF PEPPER

Schinus molle, *an evergreen tree native to the high plains of Bolivia, Peru and Chile, is better known as pink pepper or false pepper. The seeds of the fruit (peppercorns) produce an intense, aromatic aroma, similar to that of pepper, but the taste is much milder. They are used as a spice in cooking. Pink peppercorns can be used to add an exotic flavour to fish dishes and carpaccio. They can also be mixed with black, white and green pepper to produce Creole seasoning.*

ITALIAN-STYLE FISH AND CHIPS

Ingredients for 4 people
Preparation time 1 hour 5 minutes (1 hour preparation + 5 minutes cooking)

14 oz. (400 g) squid
10 1/2 oz. (300 g) aubergine
3 1/2 oz. (100 g) flour
3 1/2 oz. (100 g) semolina
1 lemon
vegetable oil
salt

Preparation

Clean and wash the aubergines, cut into chip-size pieces, season with salt and place in ice-cold water.

Leave to soak for at least half an hour.

Clean the squid, wash and remove the tentacles from the body. Cut the squid bodies into rings.

Drain the aubergines, dry, coat in flour and fry in very hot oil. Coat the squid in semolina and fry in a separate pan in very hot oil.

Drain the squid using a perforated spoon and leave to dry on kitchen roll.

Season with salt and serve in chip cones. Garnish with lemon wedges.

ENGLISH VERSION

Fish and chips is the classic dish of the English-speaking world and is widely consumed in the United Kingdom, Australia, New Zealand, South Africa and the United states. It is made from a fillet of white fish, usually cod, haddock or plaice, coated in a thick batter, fried and served with a generous portion of chips or French fries. Seasoned with salt and vinegar, fish and chips is often accompanied by peas flavoured with mint which are simmered to form a thick green lumpy soup. Fish and chips can be found in all London pubs served with a multitude of condiments ranging from from classic mayonnaise to spicy Worcester sauce. It is also eaten as street food served wrapped in a grease-absorbent cone or paper.

PRAWNS IN HAZELNUT CRUST

Ingredients for 4 people
Preparation time 28 minutes (25 minutes preparation + 3 minutes cooking)

12 prawn tails
2 egg whites
3 1/2 oz. (100 g) breadcrumbs
3 1/2 oz. (100 g) hazelnuts
vegetable oil
salt

Preparation

Shell the prawn tails and remove the gut.

Roughly chop the hazelnuts and mix with the breadcrumbs.

Coat the prawn tails in slightly beaten egg white and then the breadcrumb and hazelnut mixture.

Fr in lots of oil, drain, dry on kitchen roll and season with salt.

THE MAGICAL POWER OF HAZELNUTS

Peasant populations have always believed that hazelnuts have magical powers. They were given to newlyweds as a blessing for for future prosperity, they were inhabited by fairies, the stems were divining rods and collecting hazelnuts was a sign of fertility for the family. They were, and still are, widely used in medicine. The symbol used by pharmacists says it all: two snakes twined around a hazelnut branch. Moreover the nutritional properties of the hazelnut are legion. Hazelnuts are not only tasty and versatile but also packed with energy (628 calories for every 3 1/2 oz. [100 g] of fresh nuts and 646 for every 3 1/2 oz. [100 g] of dried nuts). They have antiseptic and anti-inflammatory properties, aid digestion, act as a mild laxative and protect the cardiovascular system. They are rich in vitamins A and E, iron, calcium and emulsin which aids the digestion of starch. They are also excellent when eaten as a dried fruit in small quantities every day.

GRILLED SQUID SALAD WITH THYME DRESSING

Ingredients for 4 people
Preparation time 1 hour 8 minutes (1 hour preparation + 8 minutes cooking)

4-5 small squid
3 1/2 tbsp. (50 ml) extra-virgin olive oil
4 sprigs thyme
1 3/4 oz. (50 g) mixed salad leaves
salt and pepper

Preparation

Clean the thyme thoroughly. Heat half the olive oil to approximately 140°F (60°C) and place the thyme leaves in the oil to infuse for approximately half an hour.

Carefully wash and clean the squid.

Brush the squid with extra-virgin olive oil, season with pepper and grill on both sides for approximately 8 minutes in total.

Slice the squid, dress with the thyme-infused oil and leave to marinate for approximately half an hour.

Dress the salad leaves with the remaining oil and a pinch of salt in four single-serving bowls. Lay the thyme-flavoured squid on top.

LIQUID GOLD

The olive tree (scientific name Olea europea) is one of the most enduring images associated with the countries in the Mediterranean basin. The fruit from the tree is pressed to make olive oil. The most highly prized is known as extra-virgin olive oil which, according to the production regulations issued by the European Union in 2003, must comply with certain specific requisites such as using only oil obtained from the first press of the fruit and containing maximum acidity of 0.8%. Extra-virgin olive oil must also have specific sensory properties including a fruity aroma and a slightly bitter, spicy taste. Due to its nutritional content and taste, extra-virgin olive oil is undoubtedly the single best oil for use in cooking. Delicious when used for dressings and excellent for frying as well as in the preservation of foods.

COUSCOUS SALAD
WITH CHICKPEAS, MUSSELS, CLAMS AND PRAWNS

Ingredients for 8 people
Preparation time 50 minutes

4 1/2 oz. (125 g) couscous, pre-cooked
3 1/2 oz. (100 g) mussels
3 1/2 oz. (100 g) clams
12 prawns
1 3/4 oz. (50 g) chickpeas, boiled
3 1/2 tbsp. (50 ml) extra-virgin olive oil
1 tsp. (2 g) parsley, chopped
1 tsp. (2 g) poppy seeds
1 garlic clove
1 chilli pepper
salt and pepper

Preparation

Pour a tablespoon of olive oil into a large frying pan and cook the garlic and chilli pepper. Clean and wash the mussels and clams and add to the frying pan. Cook over a high heat until the shellfish open and remove the shells.

De-shell and clean the prawns. Heat two tablespoons of olive oil in another frying pan, sauté the prawns and season with salt.

In a pan boil a quantity of water equal to the weight of the couscous. Place the couscous in a thick-bottomed dish. Pour the boiling water over the couscous and mix thoroughly using a wooden fork to prevent the formation of clumps. Seal the dish with cling film and leave to rest for approximately 30 minutes.

Carefully fluff the couscous, add the chopped prawns (keep one prawn to use as garnish for each serving), mussels, clams, chickpeas, chopped parsley and poppy seeds. Season with salt and pepper as necessary. Serve in small individual glasses and garnish with a drizzle of olive oil and the remaining prawns.

FROM AFRICA TO SICILY

Couscous is made from tiny grains of durum wheat semolina, although other types of cereals may be used, which are steamed. The individual grains have a diameter of 1/32 inch (1 mm) before cooking. Couscous originated in Africa but it is still unclear whether in the North or Sub-Saharan area of the continent. It is widely consumed in western Sicily particularly in the area around Trapani. Couscous is the staple food of of Morocco, Algeria and Tunisia and is served with a huge variety of meat, fish and vegetable dishes. The classic Trapani version is couscous with "ghiotta", a delicious fish soup like bouillabaisse.

BRIK STUFFED WITH ASPARAGUS AND KING PRAWNS

Ingredients for 4 people
Preparation time 1 hour (45 minutes preparation + 15 minutes cooking)

3/4 oz. (18 g) butter
3/4 oz. (20 g) all-purpose flour
5 tbsp. (75 ml) milk
2 1/2 oz. (70 g) Parmigiano Reggiano cheese, grated
8 asparagus spears
8 king prawn tails
2 tsp. (10 ml) extra-virgin olive oil
1 3/4 oz. (10 g) shallot
4 sheets brik dough
vegetable oil
salt and pepper

Preparation

Melt the butter in a small pan, add the flour and milk and bring to the boil stirring all the time. Leave to cool and add the grated Parmigiano Reggiano. Season with salt as necessary.

Peel the king prawns, remove the guts and season the tails with salt and pepper.

Wash the asparagus and remove the woody root ends. Blanch the asparagus tips in lightly salted boiling water, drain and cool in ice-cold water.

Sweat the chopped shallot with the olive oil in a frying pan. Chop the asparagus stems, add to the frying pan, season with salt and add some of the water in which the asparagus was cooked. Cook for approximately 15 minutes, blend and then sieve.

Lay out the sheets of brik dough on the worktop, spread over a layer of Parmigiano Reggiano sauce, the asparagus tips and king prawn tails and roll up the pastry.

Line a baking tray with greaseproof paper, place the brik rolls on top and cook in the oven at approximately 390°F (200°C) for 15 minutes.

Serve the brik rolls with the asparagus coulis.

ANOTHER BRIK IN THE KITCHEN

Brik is a speciality of Arab and North African cooking, particularly in Tunisia and Lebanon. Very similar to filo pastry, brik is a very light, almost intangible millefeuille with a delicate taste. It is used to make savoury pastries stuffed with vegetables, meat or fish as well as sweet pastries with fillings using honey, dried fruit or custard. Making brik dough at home is very difficult, if not almost impossible. However it can be bought easily, in very thin sheets ready for use, from speciality food shops. Brik is tasty and versatile. Today is is also very fashionable.

SWORDFISH ROULADES

Ingredients for 4 people
Preparation time 40 minutes (30 minutes preparation + 10 minutes cooking)

9 oz. (250 g) swordfish steak
1 oz. (30 g) breadcrumbs
3/4 oz. (20 g) raisins
2 tsp. (10 g) pine nuts
1/2 oz. (10 g) pistachio nuts
4 tsp. (20 ml) extra-virgin olive oil
1 lime
mixed salad leaves
oregano
salt and pepper

Preparation

Cut the swordfish steak into 4 slices and dice the remainder.

Mix the diced swordfish with the breadcrumbs, pine nuts, pistachio nuts, raisins, a pinch of oregano, salt, pepper and half the olive oil. Add the zest from half a lime.

Spread the stuffing over the slices of swordfish and roll into roulades.

Grease a baking tray with some olive oil, add the roulades and cook in the oven at 350° F (180°C) for approximately 10 minutes.

Leave the roulades to cool then cut them in half. Insert a cocktail stick with a lime segment in each piece and serve warm or at room temperature on a bed of mixed salad leaves.

SMALL SWEET GRAPES

Raisins (uvetta or uva passa in Italian) are made by drying Sultana grapes. Originally from Greece, Turkey or Iran, they take their name from the town of Sultania (Sudak) in the Crimea. The grape are small, sweet and seedless. The high concentration of sugars in raisins means they can crystallise. They are easily decrystallised by immersing them in a liquid (water, water and alcohol or fruit juice) for a few minutes. This process makes the raisins soft meaning they can be used in the preparation of pastries and savoury dishes. Raisins appear in many savoury and dessert recipes throughout Italy, particularly in Sicily, Campania, Veneto, and Liguria.

SEA BASS CARPACCIO

Ingredients for 6 people
Preparation time 20 minutes

1 sea bass (approximately 1/2 lb / 250 g)
3 limes
extra-virgin olive oil
salt and pepper
baby salad leaves

Preparation

Fillet the sea bass removing any remaining bones with tweezers and slice the two fillets very finely using a sharp knife.

Squeeze the lime juice over the fish and leave to marinate for 5 minutes. Season with salt, pepper, a dash of olive oil and serve on a bed of baby salad leaves.

A FISH WITH UNDISPUTED CULINARY FAME

Sea bass (scientific name Dicentrarchus labrax) *has a variety of names in Italian ranging from "spigola" in Central and Southern Italy to "branzino" in Northern Italy and "ragno" in Tuscany. This fish lives in the temperate waters of the Mediterranean, Black Sea and Eastern Atlantic ocean usually along the coastline. It has a long tapered body with two dorsal fins. The seven erect spikes on the main fin are probably the reason the fish is also called "spigola" in Italian, "spiga" meaning spike. On average they grow to a size of 18 to 24 inches (45-60 cm) but fully grown adults can also reach up to one and a half meters in length. The sea bass is highly esteemed in many cuisines for its fragrant and tasty white flesh. A temptation for any gourmet. Classic recipes include roast sea bass with vegetables (usually potatoes or tomato), herbs (bay leaf, parsley, sage and basil) and a dash of white wine. However the tasty white flesh of this fish make it ideal to be eaten raw, as in this tasty carpaccio recipe.*

SALMON AND DILL FISHCAKES

Ingredients for 6 people
Preparation time 50 minutes (45 minutes preparation + 5 minutes cooking)

10 1/2 oz. (300 g) salmon fillet
2 tsp. (10 ml) extra-virgin olive oil
3 1/2 oz. (100 g) sandwich loaf bread
6 1/2 tbsp. (100 ml) milk
1 egg
2 egg whites
7 oz. (200 g) breadsticks
1 tbsp. (2 g) parsley, chopped
flour
dill
vegetable oil
salt and pepper

Preparation

Season the salmon fillet with salt and pepper then cook with the olive oil in the oven at 350°F (180°C) for approximately 10 minutes.

Remove from the oven, leave to cool and then break the salmon into flakes.

In the meantime blend the breadsticks and parsley in a food processor to obtain a green breadcrumb mix.

Soak the sandwich loaf bread in the milk, wring out and chop.

In a bowl mix the salmon, bread, egg, salt, pepper and chopped dill.

Mould into small cakes, coat in flour, the slightly whisked egg white and the green breadcrumb mixture.

Heat the vegetable oil in a frying pan, fry the fishcakes for approximately 5 minutes and drain on kitchen roll.

A MEDICINAL HERB

Dill (scientific name Anethum graveolens) *is an annual herb in the celery family Apiaceae originating in the Mediterranean basin. It has been used since the time of the ancient Egyptians thanks to its medicinal properties. Dill has anti-inflammatory effects and aids digestion. It was also used as an antispasmodic, diuretic, painkiller and antiseptic. The seeds and leaves are both used in cooking, both fresh and dried, thanks to their powerful aroma which makes dill similar to fennel. It is usually used to enhance the flavor of fish dishes to increase fragrance and improve taste.*

OCTOPUS WITH CITRUS FRUITS

Ingredients for 4 people
Preparation time 20 minutes

7 oz. (200 g) cooked octopus
1 orange
1 lime
1 grapefruit
1 3/4 oz. (50 g) valerian
4 tsp. (20 ml) extra-virgin olive oil
salt and pepper

Preparation

Peel the orange, lime and grapefruit and remove the pith. Cut the citrus fruits into segments to add to the salad. Do this by slipping a knife between each segment and the connective membrane. Repeat this for all the segments.

When you have finished use your hands to squeeze the juice from the remaining part of the citrus fruits into a bowl. Add the salt, pepper and oil to the citrus juice and whisk to make a dressing for the salad.

Cut the octopus into small pieces, add some of the citrus dressing and season with salt and pepper.

Wash the valerian and place in 4 small glasses. Add the octopus, citrus fruit segments and then drizzle the dressing on top.

Garnish as required, for example using dehydrated citrus wheels and fried spaghetti.

A POWERFUL ALLY FOR THE WAISTLINE

Research has shown that eating grapefruit, particularly the red variety rather than the yellow or pink ones, as part of a calorie-controlled diet can assist in the slimming process. Grapefruit is packed full of vitamins A and C, fibre and minerals and greatly reduces appetite when eaten at the start of a meal. That's not all. It also acts as an enzyme in the burning of calories.

GRILLED SALMON WITH RED PEPPER COULIS

Ingredients for 4 people
Preparation time 49-50 minutes (45 minutes preparation + 4-5 minutes cooking)

7 oz. (200 g) salmon fillet
1 firm and fleshy red pepper
vegetable stock
oil to grease the grill
salt and pepper

Preparation

Wash the red pepper and cook on a grill or in a clean and greased griddle pan for approximately 15-20 minutes, turning when the skin starts to burn.

When ready (soft but not overcooked), remove from the grill and place in sealed freezer bag. The steam makes the red pepper easier to peel.

Remove the skin and seeds and blend the pepper with some vegetable stock and a pinch of salt.

Cut the salmon fillet into cubes (approximately 3/4 to 1 1/4 inch [2-3 cm]) and season lightly with salt and pepper.

Cook the salmon in a clean and greased griddle pan for 4-5 minutes

Serve with the red pepper coulis.

VARIED AND WIDELY APPRECIATED

Peppers are the fruit of the Capsicum annuum, a plant belonging to the family Solanaceae. They first appeared on European dining tables during the first half of the sixteenth century having been taken to the old world from Central and South America by the Spanish. Their botanic uniformity makes peppers suitable for a whole range of cooking and preservation methods. Both mild and spicy peppers are an integral part of the Italian gastronomic tradition and they are widely eaten throughout the entire country. Peppers are not only tasty but also very nutritious. They are rich in vitamin C (especially when eaten raw) and potassium. They also contain beta carotene and other carotenoids which are absorbed better by the body when eaten with lipids, for example a good quality extra-virgin olive oil.

STUFFED SARDINE LOLLIPOPS

Ingredients for 12 lollipops
Preparation time 33 minutes (30 minutes preparation + 3 minutes cooking)

24 sardines
1 3/4 oz. (50 g) breadcrumbs
2 tsp. (10 g) pitted black olives
2 tsp. (10 g) pine nuts
1 tsp. (2 g) chopped parsley
1 egg white
vegetable oil
salt and pepper

Preparation

Clean the sardines by removing the head, guts and fishbone. Butterfly the sardines, rinse and dry.

Mix half the breadcrumbs with the parsley, pine nuts, chopped black olives, a pinch of salt and pepper and enough egg white to obtain a homogenous mixture.

Place half of the open sardines on the worktop and layer the stuffing on top. Place a lollipop stick in the middle and cover with the other half of the sardines.

Press lightly to make sure each lollipop is formed correctly.

Sprinkle the remaining breadcrumbs over the lollipops and fry in lots of very hot oil.

Drain, dry on kitchen roll, season with salt and serve.

A TASTY OILY FISH

Sardines belong to the Scombridae family and can be found throughout the world's oceans. The Mediterranean variety has the scientific name Sarda sarda but is also commonly known as "palamita" from the Italian for trawl line. Sardines are a pelagic fish. Marine life is divided into the pelagic zone and the benthic zone. The pelagic zone is then further divided into the neritic zone, between the shoreline and the edge of the continental shelf, and the oceanic zone which extends beyond the continental shelf. This means that sardines mainly inhabit deeper waters but can also be found in coastal areas. Sardines have a spindle-shaped body with a pointed head. They are a metallic blue colour with black or grey slanting stripes on their back, silver sides and a mother of pearl belly. They can grow up to 32 inches (80 cm) in length and up to 22 lbs. (10 kg) in weight.

SALMON EN CROUTE WITH SPINACH AND POPPY SEEDS

Ingredients for 4 people
Preparation time 40 minutes (20 minutes preparation + 20 minutes cooking)

9 oz. (250 g) salmon fillet
9 oz. (250 g) fresh spinach
7 oz. (200 g) puff pastry
4 tsp. (20 ml) extra-virgin olive oil
1 egg
1 garlic clove
poppy seeds
salt and pepper

Preparation

Wash the spinach.

Peel and lightly crush the garlic. Heat the extra-virgin olive oil in a pan and add the garlic.

After a few seconds add the spinach. Season with salt and pepper and cover. Cook the spinach for a maximum of 3-4 minutes, remove the cover and the garlic.

Skin the salmon fillet and remove any remaining bones. Cut the fillet in half lengthways and lightly season with salt and pepper.

Use a rolling pin to roll the puff pastry into a rectangle with a thickness of approximately 1/16 inch (2 mm). Use a fork to prick holes in the dough and brush the pastry with egg wash.

Place one of the two salmon fillets on the pastry, cover with spinach and then lay the other salmon fillet on top. Wrap the pastry around the salmon to enclose it fully. Brush the surface with the remaining egg wash and sprinkle on the poppy seeds.

Line a baking tray with greaseproof paper, put the salmon in and bake in the oven at 390°F (200°C) for approximately 18-20 minutes.

When the salmon en croute is ready, remove from the oven and allow to cool for 5 minutes before cutting into slices.

MINERALISING, BUT LESS THAN IT SEEMS

The best advert for spinach is undoubtedly Popeye who has been using it since 1929 to acquire super strength. And it's true, this vegetable is mineralising, nutritious and helps combat anaemia. However scientific research has shown that, even though spinach contains more iron than any other vegetable (2.9 mml per 3 1/2 oz [100 g]), 95% of this mineral remains unused by the body due to the presence of oxalic acid, a substance which limits the bioavailability of minerals contained in green leaf vegetables.

MUSSEL KEBABS
WITH COURGETTE AND SMOKED BACON

Ingredients for 6-8 people
Preparation time 50 minutes (45 minutes preparation + 5 minutes cooking)

2.2 lbs (1 kg mussels)
2 courgettes
2 3/4 oz. (80 g) smoked bacon, sliced
1 garlic clove
1 chilli pepper
4 tsp. (20 ml) extra-virgin olive oil
salt

Preparation

Clean the mussels thoroughly under running cold water.

Wash the courgettes and slice thinly using a mandolin.

Sauté briefly on both sides in a non-stick frying pan with a drizzle of olive oil and season with salt.

Peel the garlic. Heat the whole clove of garlic in a frying pan with the olive oil and chilli pepper, add the mussels and cook until open. Remove the mussels from their shells.

Wrap half the mussels in the courgette slices and the other half in the slices of smoked bacon.

Thread the mussels onto wooden skewers alternating those wrapped in courgette and those wrapped in bacon.

Cook in the oven at 350°F (180°C) for 5 minutes and serve. The kebabs can also be served at room temperature if you prefer.

TASTIER IN MONTHS WITHOUT AN "R"

The Mediterranean mussel (scientific name Mytilus galloprovincialis) *is a species of bivalve, a marine mollusc in the family Mytilidae. Depending on the geographic area, mussels are known by various names in Italian including "muscolo", "peocio", "mosciolo", "dattero nero", "dente di vecchia" and "cozza". They are rich in iron (5.8 mml for every 100 g) and used in lots of different recipes. Mussels are extremely versatile and can be cooked in a marinara sauce (in a frying pan with white wine and herbs), baked in the oven with a parsley, garlic and olive oil gratin topping, fried in batter or cooked on a kebab. Of course we shouldn't forget the local Neapolitan tradition which states that mussels should only be eaten during months without an "r" as this is when they are at their meatiest and tastiest.*

SWORDFISH AND LIME KEBABS

Ingredients for 8 kebabs
Preparation time 23 minutes (15 minutes preparation + 8 minutes cooking)

6 1/2 oz. (180 g) swordfish steak
2 limes
1 spring onion
4 tsp. (20 ml) extra-virgin olive oil
salt and pepper

Preparation

Remove the skin from the swordfish, trim and cut into eight pieces.

Wash the limes and cut off the ends. Cut each lime into four wedges. Squeeze the juice from the ends of the limes. Make a dressing using the lime juice, olive oil, salt and pepper.

Clean the spring onion and cut into sixteen pieces.

Alternately thread the ingredients onto the skewers starting with a lime wedge, a piece of spring onion, a piece of swordfish and then another piece of spring onion. Cook on a well-greased grill, brushing over the lime dressing, for approximately 8 minutes.

THE PERFUME OF A SWEET LIME

The lime, known in Italian as "limetta", is a citrus fruit of the Rutaceae family. This dainty fruit, almost like a cross between a lemon and a citron, is oval or round and has thin skin. Limes are harvested when still slightly green because they are tastier and juicer. Left to mature the fruit turns yellowy orange. Lime flesh is particularly fragrant and bitter because it contains 6% citric acid. Unlike other citrus fruits limes grow best in tropical climates and therefore is only cultivated in Egypt in the Mediterranean basin. Rarely consumed as fresh fruit, limes are often used in cooking instead of lemons which are less aromatic but contain more vitamin C. Lime improves the flavour of fruit salad and fish recipes. The lime, known in Italian as "limetta", is a citrus fruit of the Rutaceae family. This dainty fruit, almost like a cross between a lemon and cedar fruit, is oval or round and has thin skin. Limes are harvested when still slightly green because they are tastier and juicer. Left to mature the fruit turns yellowy orange. Lime flesh is particularly fragrant and bitter because it contains 6% citric acid. Unlike other citrus fruits limes grow best in tropical climates and therefore is only cultivated in Egypt in the Mediterranean basin. Rarely consumed as fresh fruit, limes are often used in cooking instead of lemons which are less aromatic but contain more vitamin C. Lime improves the flavour of fruit salad and fish recipes.

SALMON AND SOLE PINWHEELS

Ingredients for 4 people
Preparation time 57 minutes (45 minutes preparation + 12 minutes cooking)

1 sole
5 1/2 oz. (150 g) salmon fillet
2 slices sandwich loaf bread
3 1/2 tbsp. (50 ml) cream
1 egg white
3/4 oz. (20 g) pistachio nuts
salt and pepper

Preparation

Peel the pistachio nuts by blanching them in boiling water for a few seconds so the outer membrane comes ways easily when rubbing the nuts between your fingers.

Drain, peel and dry using kitchen roll.

Remove the crust from the bread and soak in a bowl with the cream.

Use a boning knife to fillet the sole. Trim the salmon, remove any skin and bones then dice.

Blend the soaked bread, cream and diced salmon in a food processor making sure all the ingredients are very cold. Season with salt and pepper.

Put a sheet of cling film on the worktop and place the sole fillets on the film so they are right up against each other. Lightly season with salt and pepper. Use a palette knife to spread the salmon filling on the sole. Sprinkle over the pistachio nuts and roll up using the film to help you.

Remove the film and wrap the roulade in tin foil.

Place in a pan of boiling water and simmer for approximately 12 minutes.

Leave to cool and then slice using a very sharp knife.

Serve on toast or accompanied with a side salad.

SMILING SEEDS

In all probability pistachio nuts were the first snack in human history. They are the seeds from the tree of the same name which is part of the Anacardiaceae family. Pistachio nuts with their sweet and fragrant flavour are packed full of energy. They are also rich in vitamins A and B, protein, Omega-6 fatty acids and mineral salts. Pistachios originated in Syria where they are called "smiling seeds" thanks to their half-open shell. According to legend they were grown in the Hanging Gardens of Babylon and very much appreciated by the Queen of Sheeba.

FISH TARTARE

Ingredients for 6-8 people
Preparation time 96 hours 30 minutes
(30 minutes preparation + 96 hours freezing

5 1/2 oz. (150 g) salmon fillet
5 1/2 oz. (150 g) greater amberjack or sea bass fillet
1 tomato
1/2 avocado
chives, raspberries
salt and pepper

Preparation

Freeze the fish for at least 96 hours at 0°F (-18°C) to kill off any anisakis.

Peel the tomato, remove the seeds and dice.

Stone, peel and dice the avocado.

Remove the skin from the fish. Remove any remaining bones using tweezers. Trim and dice the fillets. Season with salt and pepper.

Build the fish tartare with the help of a small mould. Make a bed of avocado and layer the salmon on top. Use the tomato as the bed for the greater amberjack or sea bass.

Garnish with fresh raspberries, chives or anything else that takes your fancy.

HIGH-QUALITY LEAN FISH

The greater amberjack (scientific name Seriola dumerili) is a marine fish in the family Ca-rangidae. It is native to the Mediterranean Sea, Pacific Ocean, Atlantic Ocean and the Indian coasts. Fully grown adults can reach up to 81 inches (2 m) in length and exceed 220 lbs. (100 kg) in weight. They are silver-blue with a golden side line, with a brown band crossing over the eye area. The flesh of this fish is tasty as well as being rich in protein and Omega 3 fatty acids. The greater amberjack is widely used in cooking to make carpaccio, tartares, fish steaks and light, tasty pasta sauces.

PRAWN AND ARTICHOKE SAVOURY TART

Ingredients for 12 portions
Preparation time 2 hours 20 minutes
(1 hour preparation + 1 hour resting + 20 minutes cooking)

FOR THE SHORT CRUST PASTRY
7 oz. (200 g) all-purpose flour
3 1/2 oz. (100 g) butter
1 3/4-2 tbsp. (25-30 ml) water
1/4 tsp. (4 g) salt

FOR THE FILLING
3 artichokes

7 oz. (200 g) prawn tails
1 cup (250 ml) cream
2 egg yolks
1 3/4 tbsp. (25 ml) extra-virgin olive oil
3/4 oz. (20 g) Parmigiano Reggiano
cheese, grated
1 garlic clove
salt and pepper

Preparation

For the short crust pastry cut the butter into small pieces and mix with the flour to form a "sandy" heterogeneous dough.

Add the salt and cold water and mix to obtain a uniform dough without over-kneading.

Wrap the dough in cling film and leave to stand in the fridge for at least an hour.

In the meantime clean the prawn tails and cut into three pieces. Clean the artichokes and slice finely.

Peel the garlic. Heat the oil in a frying pan, add the garlic and artichokes and sauté for a couple of minutes over a medium heat. Add the prawns, season with salt and pepper and continue cooking for a few seconds. Remove the garlic

Roll out the short crust pastry to a thickness of approximately 1/16 inch (2 mm). Line a quiche tin with greaseproof paper and then the pastry. Use a fork to prick holes in the dough and then pour in the prawn and artichoke mixture.

In a bowl whisk the cream with the egg yolks, Parmigiano Reggiano and a pinch of salt and pepper. Add the mixture to the quiche tin and bake in the oven at 350°F (180°C) for approximately 20 minutes.

Remove from the oven, leave to cool and cut into squares.

A TASTY THISTLE

The globe artichoke (scientific name Cynara cardunculus var. scolymus) is a plant in the family Asteraceae. Originally a wild, perennial plant, artichokes were first cultivated in Sicily during the first century AD. Widely used throughout Italy, it is especially popular in Rome where it is a main ingredient in many local specialities. The two most famous Roman artichoke dishes are "carciofi alla romana" or roman-style artichokes, made by stewing the vegetable in olive oil and vegetable stock with parsley, garlic and mint, and "carciofo alla giudia" or "Jewish-style artichokes" where the vegetable is fried whole in olive oil. Other favourites include artichokes fried in batter and raw artichoke salad.

PAUPIETTES OF MONKFISH AND BACON

Ingredients for 4 people
Preparation time 26-27 minutes
(20 minutes preparation + 6-7 minutes cooking)

9 oz. (250 g) monkfish
2 oz. (60 g) bacon
4 tsp. (20 ml) extra-virgin olive oil
balsamic vinegar
salt and pepper

Preparation

Clean the monkfish, remove the skin and use a sharp knife to remove the two fillets from the backbone. Cut into pieces (approximately 1 1/4 inches [3 cm]), season with salt and pepper and then wrap the bacon around the monkfish.

Seal in a hot frying pan with a dash of olive oil and cook in the oven at 350°F (180°C) for 6-7 minutes.

Serve with a balsamic vinegar garnish.

A SPECIAL GIFT

Traditional balsamic vinegar from Modena – not to be confused with balsamic vinegar from Modena which is actually a wine vinegar – is one of the world's most famous and popular Italian gastronomic products. A traditional product of the Emilia region, it is made from the cooked must of grapes exclusively from the provinces of Modena and Reggio Emilia. The fermentation, acetification and ageing process must last for at least twelve years. The product has its roots in ancient Roman times but the first official records date back to 1046. Balsamic vinegar was highly esteemed at the court of the ruling House of Este already at the beginning of the thirteenth century. It was very much considered an aristocratic food for which only nobles were worthy. Over the centuries it became customary to present balsamic vinegar inside small silver bottles as gifts during ceremonies and on other special occasions. For example, in 1792 Duke Ercole III of Este sent a jar of traditional balsamic vinegar from Modena to Frankfurt for the coronation of Francis II as Holy roman Emperor.

TERRINE OF GREATER AMBERJACK, PRAWNS AND SAVOY CABBAGE

Ingredients for 6-8 portions
Preparation time 1 hour 30 minutes (1 hour preparation + 30 minutes cooking)

5 1/2 oz. (150 g) greater amberjack fillet
3 1/2 oz. (100 g) prawn tails
1 egg white
4 tbsp. (60 g) cream
1/2 oz. (10 g) butter
4 Savoy cabbage leaves
1/2 oz. (15 g) pistachio nuts, shelled
1 tsp. (2 g) pink peppercorns
salt and pepper

Preparation

Clean the prawn tails and season with salt and pepper.

In the meantime blend the greater amberjack, egg white and cream in a food processor and season with salt and pepper. Make sure all the ingredients are cold (straight from the fridge). Mix in the pistachio nuts and pink peppercorns.

Blanch the Savoy cabbage leaves in boiling salted water, drain and place in ice-cold water to cool. Use three of the leaves to line a terrine greased with butter.

Pour the fish mixture into the terrine and place the prawns in the middle. Cover with the fourth Savoy cabbage leaf.

Cook in the oven in a bain-marie at 300°F (150°C) for 30 minutes. Leave to cool and slice.

A RICH, TASTY VEGETABLE

Savoy cabbage (scientific name Brassica oleracea var. sabauda L.*) is a variety of Chinese kale. It is shaped like a ball and is green or red-violet in colour. The leaves are wrinkled and corrugated and have distinctive ribs. The Savoy cabbage is yellow white on the inside. This vegetable has ancient origins, is cultivated throughout Northern and Central Italy and is used in numerous traditional Italian cooking recipes. Rice and Savoy cabbage with pork ribs from Piacenza, bread and Savoy cabbage soup from Piedmont, pizzoccheri (type of pasta made with buckwheat) from the Valtellina and the meaty cassoeula stew from Lombardy are just a few of the many varied uses for this vegetable. Savoy cabbage can also be used to make tasty rolls which can be served as an appetiser or with an aperitif during the winter months.*

COCKTAILS

TEXT BY
GIANFRANCO DI NISO
DAVIDE MANZONI

PHOTOGRAPHS
FABIO PETRONI

The aperitifs in this book have been chosen according to a variety of criteria: the majority are drinks that have been famous for decades now where the skill of bartenders around the world has lain in being able to replicate the original recipe (we are speaking of the Negroni or Martini cocktail or the Manhattan). Another criterion used in the choice was that of selecting aperitif cocktails which, although from the point of view of ingredients are not exactly part of the family, have become 'musts' over the last few decades: we are talking about the famous Mojito, the Margarita or Caipiroska. Other drinks are those which on the back of fashion have once again become really well-known throughout the world: the Spritz, the Apple Martini or the Garibaldi (famous in Germany and America by the name of Campari Orange). The selection also finds space for that section of the public which during aperitifs prefers to opt for less alcoholic drinks that are richer in fruits (like the famous Rossini, or the more jet-set apple Martini). A final but no less important criterion was to suggest drinks that are simple to replicate and adapt to various foods, with ingredients that can be easily found, in such a way that readers will be able to prepare an excellent aperitif even if they are not talented bartenders.

AMERICANO

Ingredients for 1 cocktail
Campari 3 cl (1 oz)
red vermouth 3 cl (1 oz)
soda water
or sparkling water
3 cl (1 oz)

% ALC/VOL: 9.7 • CALORIES: 57

Origins and oddities
Legend has it that this drink was created in
Italy during the fascist regime in the 1930s,
and that its name was chosen to honor the
achievements of the boxer Primo Carnera,
who in 1933, became world heavyweight
champion by winning a bout at Madison
Square Garden in New York.

Preparation
Measure 3 cl (1 oz) of Campari in a
graduated cylinder and pour in a low
tumbler filled with ice. Repeat with 3 cl (1 oz)
of red vermouth. Fill almost to the brim with
3 cl (1 oz) of soda water or sparkling water.
Gently stir everything with a long-handled
spoon and serve, garnished with 1/2 a slice
of orange and lemon peel.

Excellent as an aperitif.

APPLE MARTINI

Ingredients for 1 cocktail
dry vodka 4,5 cl (1 1/2 oz)
apple liqueur 2 cl (2/3 oz)
Cointreau 2 cl (2/3 oz)

% ALC/VOL: 25.4 • CALORIES: 188

Origins and oddities
One of the most popular variations of the
classic Martini Cocktail was created in New
York in the late 1980s and soon became very
popular among younger drinkers.

Preparation
Measure 4,5 cl (1 1/2 oz) of vodka in a
graduated cylinder and pour into a shaker.
Repeat with 2 cl (2/3 oz) of apple liqueur and
2 cl (2/3 oz) of Cointreau. Add ice cubes and
stir for a few seconds. Pour into a cup
pre-chilled in the freezer and serve.

*Usually served as an aperitif, it can easily be
enjoyed throughout the day.*

BELLINI

Ingredients for 1 cocktail
peach puree 3 cl (1 oz)
sparkling brut or champagne
6 cl (2 oz)

% ALC/VOL: 5.5 • CALORIES: 58

Origins and oddities
This famous cocktail was created in 1948
by a bartender at Harry's Bar in Venice. The
occasion was an exhibition of paintings of
Giambellino (real name Giovanni Bellini).

Preparation
Measure 3 cl (1 oz) of the peach puree in a
graduated cylinder and pour into a cup
pre-chilled in the freezer.
Fill almost to the brim with 6 cl
(2 oz) of fresh sparkling brut or
champagne. Stir gently with a
long-handled spoon and serve.

An aperitif par excellence.

BITTER MOJITO

Ingredients for 1 cocktail
Campari 4,5 cl (1 1/2 oz)
fresh orange 1/4
white sugar or cane sugar
about 20 g (about 1 1/2 tbsp)
sparkling brut 6 cl (2 oz)
fresh mint 7 g (1/4 oz,
about 7-10 fresh leaves)

% ALC/VOL: 13 • CALORIES: 180

Origins and oddities
This variation on the classic Mojito was
presented for the first time in 2007 during the
"Metamorfosi Mojito" competition in Rimini.

Preparation
Cut 1/4 an orange into cubes. Put the
orange cubes in a tall tumbler and add
about 20 g (about 1 1/2 tbsp) of white sugar.
Grind everything with a pestle until you have
a paste. Add 7-10 fresh mint leaves (about 7
g – 1/4 oz) and press lightly against the sides
of the tumbler. Fill the glass with crushed
ice and add 4,5 cl (1 1/2 oz) of Campari
(measured in a graduated cylinder). Fill
almost to the brim with 6 cl (2 oz) of fresh
sparkling brut and mix everything with a
long-handled spoon, so that the ingredients
are well blended. Serve, garnished with 1
nice sprig of fresh mint and 2 long straws.

Excellent as an aperitif.

BLOODY MARIA

Ingredients for 1 cocktail
tequila 4,5 cl (1 1/2 oz)
tomato juice 9 cl (3 oz)
lemonjuice 2 cl (2/3 oz)
spices (salt, pepper, tabasco,
Worcestershire sauce,
jalapeño pepper)

% ALC/VOL: 15.8 • CALORIES: 147

Origins and oddities
A cocktail that pays homage to the more
famous Bloody Mary, this Mexican variation
makes two changes from the British
mainstay: tequila in place of vodka and the
addition of jalapeño pepper.

Preparation
Measure 4,5 cl (1 1/2 oz) of tequila in a
graduated cylinder and pour into a high
tumbler. Repeat with 2 cl (2/3 oz) of lemon
juice and 9 cl (3 oz) of tomato juice. Add
salt, pepper, a few sprinkles of tabasco,
Worcestershire sauce, jalapeño pepper
and some ice cubes. Mix the Ingredients
thoroughly with a long-handled spoon and
serve, garnished with 1 slice of avocado, 1
celery stick (optional) and 2 long straws.

*Perfect for any cocktail hour, it is good
throughout the evening.*

BRONX

Ingredients for 1 cocktail
gin 3 cl (1 oz)
red vermouth 2 cl (2/3 oz)
dry vermouth 2 cl (2/3 oz)
orange juice 2 cl (2/3 oz)

% ALC/VOL: 14.8 • CALORIES: 121

Origins and oddities
The story goes that Joseph S. Sormani,
a bartender of Italian descent, at the
beginning of the 1900s introduced this
drink created in Philadelphia in his Bronx
neighborhood. It was an instant success.

Preparation
Measure 3 cl (1 oz) of gin in a graduated
cylinder and pour in a
shaker. Repeat with 2 cl (2/3
oz) of red vermouth, 2 cl
(2/3 oz) of dry vermouth and
2 cl (2/3 oz) of orange juice.
Add some ice cubes and shake
vigorously for a few seconds.
Pour into a cup pre-chilled in the
freezer and serve.

Bronx is an excellent aperitif.

CAIPIRINHA

Ingredients for 1 cocktail
lime 1/2
white or cane
sugar about 20 g
(about 1 1/2 tbsp)
cachaça 5-6 cl (2 oz)

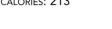

% ALC/VOL: **18.9**
CALORIES: **213**

Origins and oddities
At the beginning of the 1900s, farmers in Brazil (the "caipira") used to drink this now famous drink during cultivation.

Preparation
Place 1/2 a lime, cut into cubes, and about 20 g (about 1 1/2 tbsp) of sugar in a low tumbler and, using a pestle, crush it all up until you have a paste. Fill a glass with crushed ice and pour 5-6 cl (2 oz) of cachaça (measured in a graduated cylinder). Stir for a few seconds with a long handled spoon to mix the best Ingredients. Serve, garnished with 2 short straws.

Perfect for an after-dinner drink, it is an exceptional evening aperitif.

CAIPIROSKA

Ingredients for 1 cocktail
dry vodka 6 cl (2 oz)
lime 1/2
white or cane sugar
about 20 g
(about 1 1/2 tbsp)

% ALC/VOL: **18.9**
CALORIES: **225**

Origins and oddities
A modern reinterpretation of the famous Brazilian Caipirinha, which, over the years, has become one of the most popular drinks in the world.

Preparation
Place 1/2 a lime, cut into cubes, in a low tumbler and add about 20 g (about 1 1/2 tbsp) of sugar. With a pestle, crush it all up until you have a paste. Fill the glass with crushed ice and pour in 6 cl (2 oz) of vodka (measured in a graduated cylinder). Stir for a few seconds with a long-handled spoon, so that the Ingredients are well blended. Serve, garnished with 2 short straws.

A great drink to be enjoyed at all hours of the day, it is much loved by younger drinkers and very popular during Happy Hour.

CANNES

Ingredients for 1 cocktail
brandy or cognac 2 cl (2/3 oz)
dry vermouth 3 cl (1 oz)
Campari 2 cl (2/3 oz)
orange juice 2 cl (2/3 oz)

% ALC/VOL: **16.5** • CALORIES: **103**

Origins and oddities
This cocktail was served in France in the 1960s at events organized to welcome filmmakers and actors to the Cannes Film Festival.

Preparation
Measure 2 cl (2/3 oz) of cognac or brandy in a graduated cylinder and pour into a shaker. Repeat with 3 cl (1 oz) of dry vermouth, 2 cl (2/3 oz) of Campari and 2 cl (2/3 oz) of orange juice. Add ice cubes and shake vigorously for a few seconds. Pour into a cup pre-chilled in the freezer and serve, garnished with 1/2 an orange slice, and 2 cherries.

Perfect as an aperitif.

CHEROKEE

Ingredients for 1 cocktail
gin 3 cl (1 oz)
Campari 2 cl (2/3 oz)
orange juice 7 cl (2 1/2 oz)
grapefruit juice 3 cl (1 oz)
grenadine syrup
1 cl (1/4 oz)

% ALC/VOL: 13.4
CALORIES: 129

Origins and oddities
A modern drink, the Cherokee's amber color
is a reminder of the dark skin tones of the
cherokee Indians.

Preparation
Measure 3 cl (1 oz) of gin in a graduated
cylinder and pour into a tall tumbler
filled with ice. Repeat with 2 cl (2/3 oz) of
Campari, 7 cl (2 1/2 oz) of orange juice, 3
cl (1 oz) of grapefruit juice and 1 cl (1/4 oz)
of grenadine syrup. Mix the Ingredients
well with a long-handled spoon and serve,
garnished with 2 long straws, 2 cocktail
cherries, 1 sprig of mint and 2 orange slices.

*This long drink is enjoyed around the world,
most especially at Happy Hour.*

COCKTAIL CHAMPAGNE

Ingredients for 1 cocktail
brandy or cognac 2 cl (2/3 oz)
champagne or sparkling brut
6 cl (2 oz)
sugar 1 lump
Grand Marnier 2 cl (2/3 oz)

% ALC/VOL: 17 • CALORIES: 177

Origins and oddities
Created as an aperitif in the early 1920s
in France, is among the most popular
sparkling wine cocktails in the world.

Preparation
Place 1 lump of sugar in a cup pre-chilled in
the freezer and add 2 cl (2/3 oz) of brandy
or cognac and 2 cl (2/3 oz) of Grand Marnier
(measured in a graduated cylinder). Repeat
with 6 cl (2 oz) of champagne or sparkling
brut and mix gently with a long-handled
spoon. Serve, garnished with 1/2 an orange
slice and 1 cherry.

*A sophisticated drink for cocktail hour,
it is nevertheless good for any time of day.*

COSMOPOLITAN

Ingredients for 1 cocktail
dry vodka 3 cl (1 oz)
Cointreau 2 cl (2/3 oz)
lemon juice 1,5 cl (1/2 oz)
cranberry juice 3 cl (1 oz)

% ALC/VOL: 15.8 • CALORIES: 136

Origins and oddities
It has been said that in 1987, a famous
Miami bartender named Cheryl Cook
created a cocktail that would satisfy the
taste of women.

Preparation
Measure 3 cl (1 oz) of dry vodka in a
graduated cylinder and pour into a shaker.
Repeat with 2 cl (2/3 oz)
of Cointreau, 1,5 cl (1/2 oz)
of lemon juice and 3 cl (1 oz)
of cranberry juice.
Add some ice cubes and shake
vigorously for a few seconds.
Pour into a cocktail glass
pre-chilled in the freezer
and serve.

*Recommended for the evenings
or during Happy Hour.*

FRENCH KISS

Ingredients for 1 cocktail
Aperol 6 cl (2 oz)
Campari 2 cl (1/2 oz)
Grand Marnier
2 cl (1/2 oz)
A.C.E. (orange/carrot/
lemon) ice cream 2 tbsp

% ALC/VOL: 14.5
CALORIES: 221

Origins and oddities
A drink created in the 1990s by a Parisian
barlady who was hopelessly in love with
a Spanish painter who used to come
to her ice cream shop in Montmartre.

Preparation
Measure 60 ml (1/4 cup) of Aperol in a
graduated cylinder and pour into a blender.
Repeat with 20 ml (4 tsp) of Grand Marnier
and 10 ml (2 tsp) of Campari. Add 2 tbsp of
A.C.E ice cream and 1/2 a low tumbler of
crushed ice. Blend for 15-20 seconds and
pour into a tall tumbler. Serve, garnished
with 1/2 a slice of pineapple, 2 cherries and
2 long straws.

A delicious aperitif.

GARIBALDI

Ingredients for 1 cocktail
Campari 6 cl (2 oz)
orange juice (preferably
red) 9 cl (3 oz)

% ALC/VOL: 13.8 • CALORIES: 79

Origins and oddities
This cocktail was created in the 1960s, and
its name is inspired by the famous head
scarf worn by Giuseppe Garibaldi.

Preparation
Measure 6 cl (2 oz) of Campari in a
graduated cylinder and pour into a tall
tumbler filled with ice. Repeat with 9 cl (3 oz)
of orange juice. Stir for a few seconds with
a long-handled spoon and serve, garnished
with 1 orange slice and 2 long straws.

*An excellent aperitif that can be enjoyed at
all hours of the day.*

ITALIAN BITTER

Ingredients for 1 cocktail
Aperol 3 cl (1 oz)
Campari 1 cl (1/4 oz)
peach vodka 2 cl (1/2 oz)
Sanbittèr

% ALC/VOL: 8.5 • CALORIES: 92

Origins and oddities
This drink was also presented for the first
time in Rimini in 2005 at the international
bartending competition whose theme
was the conception of innovative aperitif
cocktails.

Preparation
Measure 30 ml (2 tbsp) of Aperol in a
graduated cylinder and pour into a shaker.
Repeat with 20 ml (4 tsp)
of vodka and 10 ml (2 tsp)
of Campari.
Stir for a few seconds and
pour into a tall tumbler filled
with ice, then fill almost to
the brim with Sanbittèr.
Stir gently with long-handled
spoon and serve, garnished
with 1/2 a slice of orange,
2 cherries and 2 long
straws.

Excellent as an aperitif.

KIR ROYAL

Ingredients for 1 cocktail
Crème de Cassis 2 cl (2/3 oz)
champagne or sparkling brut
(classic method) 9 cl (3 oz)

% ALC/VOL: 10.5
CALORIES: 122

Origins and oddities
An evolution from the classic Kir, it was
created in Paris in the Belle Époque.

Preparation
Measure 2 cl (2/3 oz) of Crème de Cassis in
a graduated cylinder and pour into a cup
pre-chilled in the freezer. Fill almost to the
brim with 9 cl (3 oz) of fresh champagne
or sparkling brut. Stir gently with a long-
handled spoon and serve.

*An elegant aperitif that can be served
throughout the day.*

MANHATTAN

Ingredients for 1 cocktail
canadian whiskey 6 cl (2 oz)
red vermouth 3 cl (1 oz)
angostura a few drops

% ALC/VOL: 22.7
CALORIES: 196

Origins and oddities
Legend has it that Winston Churchill's
mother was the person to suggest the
recipe for this famous drink, guiding one
of the bartenders at the Manhattan Club in
New York in the 1920s.

Preparation
Measure 6 cl (2 oz) of Canadian Whiskey
in a graduated cylinder and pour into a
glass carafe. Repeat with 3 cl (1 oz) of red
vermouth. Add a few drops of angostura
and ice cubes. Mix everything together
with a long-handled spoon. Pour into a cup
pre-chilled in the freezer, holding the ice
back with the spoon so that it does not end
up in the cup. Serve, garnished with 1 or 2
cherries.

*One of the best apertifs, it is very good
throughout the evening.*

MARGARITA

Ingredients for 1 cocktail
tequila 4,5 cl (1 1/2 oz)
Cointreau 2,5 cl (3/4 oz)
lemon or lime juice
2 cl (2/3 oz)

% ALC/VOL: 22.3 • CALORIES: 157

Origins and oddities
The most accepted legend
about the birth of the Margarita goes back
to the mid-'30s, when a man named Danny
Tergete mixed tequila, Cointreau and lemon
juice on the day of his brother's wedding. He
would name his creation Margarita, in honor
of the bride, his sister-in-law.

Preparation
Measure 4,5 cl (1 1/2 oz) of tequila in a
graduated cylinder and pour into a shaker.
Repeat with 2,5 cl 3/4 oz) of Cointreau
and 2 cl (2/3 oz) of lemon or lime juice.
Add ice cubes and shake vigorously for
a few seconds. Rub the rim of a "margarita
glass" (a stem glass) with the rind of
a lemon or lime, then dip the glass in salt
and spin. Pour and serve.

*The Margarita can be a refreshing cocktail
at all hours of the day, however, it is
especially recommended for Happy Hour.*

MARTINI COCKTAIL

Ingredients for 1 cocktail
gin 8 cl (2 1/2 oz)
dry vermouth 1 cl (1/4 oz)

% ALC/VOL: 26.7
CALORIES: 188

Origins and oddities
A well-known legend regarding this cocktail recounts the tale of an Italian bartender (with the surname Martini) who emigrated to the United States and created this drink in 1910 in honor of John D. Rockefeller, a frequent visitor to Martini's bar.

Preparation
Measure 8 cl (2 1/2 oz) of gin in a graduated cylinder and pour into a transparent pitcher. Repeat with 1 cl (1/4 oz) of dry vermouth and add several ice cubes. Stir with a long-handled spoon and pour into a cocktail glass pre-chilled in the freezer, being careful that the ice does not slide into the glass. Serve, garnished with 10 g (0.35 oz) previously rinsed green olives skewered on a long toothpick and a lemon rind.

Dry and slightly aromatic, Martini Cocktail has become the world's most popular aperitif, and is especially recommended during Happy Hour.

MIMOSA

Ingredients for 1 cocktail
orange juice 3 cl (1 oz)
sparkling brut or champagne 9 cl (3 oz)

% ALC/VOL: 7.8 • CALORIES: 96

Origins and oddities
Created in London in 1921, this drink was conceived by the imagination of Mr. Harry, the bartender at Buck's Club. The original name of this cocktail was Buck's Fizz.

Preparation
Measure 3 cl (1 oz) of orange juice in a graduated cylinder and pour into a cup pre-chilled in the freezer. Fill almost to the brim with 9 cl (3 oz) of fresh sparkling brut or champagne. Stir gently with a long-handled spoon and serve.

An excellent aperitif that can be enjoyed at all hours of the day.

MERCEDES

Ingredients for 1 cocktail
tequila 2 cl (2/3 oz)
Aperol 7 cl (2 1/2 oz)
strawberry puree or
strawberry juice 3 cl (1 oz)
grapefruit juice 4,5 cl (1 1/2 oz)

% ALC/VOL: 12.4 • CALORIES: 107

Origins and oddities
A drink created by a bartender in Acapulco in honor of Mercedes, a beautiful Mexican girl who frequented the beaches in the area.

Preparation
Measure 2 cl (2/3 oz) of tequila in a graduated cylinder and pour into a tall tumbler filled with ice. Repeat with 7 cl (2 1/2 oz) of Aperol, 4,5 cl (1 1/2 oz) of grapefruit juice and 3 cl (1 oz) of strawberry puree or juice. Stir for a few seconds with a long-handled spoon and serve, garnished with 1/2 a slice of orange, 2 strawberries and 2 long straws.

An excellent long drink, it is recommended as an aperitif before a Mexican meal.

MOJITO

Ingredients for 1 cocktail
whitwe rum 4,5 cl (1 1/2 oz)
white sugar or cane sugar
about 20 g (about 1 1/2 tbsp)
fresh mint 7 g (1/4 oz)
lime 1/2
soda water or sparkling water
6 cl (2 oz)

% ALC/VOL: 14.2 • CALORIES: 180

Origins and oddities
The legend of this cocktail is based on the infamous pirate Francis Drake (1540-1596), who was said to have loved mixing rum, sugar and mint leaves (mint was believed to alleviate some ailments).

Preparation
Place 1/2 a lime (cut into cubes) in a tall tumbler. Add about 20 g (about 1 1/2 tbsp) of sugar and crush it all up with a pestle until you have a paste. Add 7-10 fresh mint leaves (about 7 g – 1/4 oz), pressing gently against the rest. Fill the glass with crushed (preferably) ice and add 4,5 cl (1 1/2 oz) of white rum (measured in a graduated cylinder). Fill to the rim with 6 cl (2 oz) of soda water or sparkling water and stir for a few seconds with a long-handled spoon, so that the Ingredients are well blended. Serve, garnished with 2 straws and a nice long sprig of fresh mint.

To be enjoyed at all hours of the day. Very suitable as an aperitif.

MOJITO FIDEL

Ingredients for 1 cocktail
white rum 4,5 cl (1 1/2 oz)
lime 3 cl (1 oz)
fresh mint 7 g (1/4 oz,
about 7-10 fresh leaves)
white sugar or cane sugar
about 20 g (about 1 1/2 tbsp)
lager 6 cl (2 oz)

% ALC/VOL: 16 • CALORIES: 195

Origins and oddities
The night before the attack to the Moncada barracks led by Fidel Castro, the revolutionaries celebrated the imminent battle with Mojitos prepared by a soldier. When they ran out of soda, the man decided to replace it with lager.

Preparation
Measure 4,5 cl (1 1/2 oz) of white rum in a graduated cylinder and pour in a tall tumbler. Repeat with 3 cl (1 oz) of freshly squeezed lime juice. Combine about 20 g (about 1 1/2 tbsp) of white sugar, 7-10 fresh mint leaves (about 7 g – 1/4 oz) and mix together with a long-handled spoon. Fill the glass with ice and fill almost to the brim with 6 cl (2 oz) of lager. Give a final mix and serve, garnished with 1 sprig of fresh mint and 2 long straws.

A drink that can be enjoyed throughout the evening, it is also recommended as an aperitif.

NEGRONI

Ingredients for 1 cocktail
gin 3 cl (1 oz)
red vermouth 3 cl (1 oz)
Campari 3 cl (1 oz)

% ALC/VOL: 19 • CALORIES: 123

Origins and oddities
The Negroni is an alcoholic cocktail created in the 1920s by bartender Fosco Scarselli in Florence, Italy, in honor of Count Camillo Negroni.

Preparation
Measure 3 cl (1 oz) of gin in a graduated cylinder and pour into a low tumbler filled with ice. Repeat with 3 cl (1 oz) of red vermouth, and 3 cl (1 oz) of Campari. Mix together for a few seconds with a long-handled spoon. Garnish with 1/2 an orange slice and serve.

The Negroni is the aperitif par excellence, but it can also be enjoyed throughout the evening.

NEGRONI SBAGLIATO

Ingredients for 1 cocktail
Campari 3 cl (1 oz)
red vermouth 3 cl (1 oz)
sparkling brut 3 cl (1 oz)

% ALC/VOL: **12.3**
CALORIES: **86**

Origins and oddities
The origins of this famous drink are quite
unique, as they stem from a bartender's
mistake at the Bar Basso in Milan in the
1960s. Trying to make a Negroni, he
accidentally substituted the classic gin with
sparkling brut: Negroni sbagliato means
"wrong Negroni".

Preparation
Measure in a graduated cylinder and pour
3 cl (1 oz) of Campari in a low tumbler filled
with ice and repeat with 3 cl (1 oz) of red
vermouth. Extend almost to the brim with
3 cl (1 oz) of fresh sparkling brut and stir
gently with a long-handled spoon. Serve,
garnished with 1 orange slice.

An aperitif par excellence.

NEW FRED ROSE

Ingredients for 1 cocktail
gin 3 cl (1 oz)
Mandarinetto Isolabella 3 cl (1 oz)
limoncello 1,5 cl (1/2 oz)
Campari 2 cl (2/3 oz)

% ALC/VOL: **22.5**
CALORIES: **128**

Origins and oddities
It's been said that this cocktail was created
by a bartender named Fred, in honor of
Rose, a girl he was smitten with.

Preparation
Measure 3 cl (1 oz) of gin in a graduated
cylinder and pour into a shaker. Repeat
with 3 cl (1 oz) of Mandarinetto Isolabella, 2
cl (2/3 oz) of Campari and 1,5 cl (1/2 oz) of
limoncello. Add some ice cubes and shake
vigorously for a few seconds. Pour into a
cocktail glass pre-chilled in the freezer and
serve, garnished with 1 slice of lemon or
lime and 1 cherry.

*This very refreshing drink can be enjoyed
throughout the day. Also recommended as
an aperitif.*

PALM BEACH

Ingredients for 1 cocktail
gin 4,5 cl (1 1/2 oz)
Campari 3 cl (1 oz)
pineapple juice 9 cl (3 oz)

% ALC/VOL: **20.5** • CALORIES: **153**

Origins and oddities
Created in the 1950s, the Palm Beach
seems to have been the welcome cocktail
of exclusive seaside resorts located on the
Atlantic coast of Florida.

Preparation
Measure 4,5 cl (1 1/2 oz) of gin in a
graduated cylinder and pour into a
shaker. Repeat with 3 cl
(1 oz) of Campari and 9 cl (3 oz)
of pineapple juice. Add ice
cubes and shake vigorously
for a few seconds.
Pour the drink into a tall
tumbler filled with ice
and serve, garnished with
1/2 a slice of pineapple,
2 cocktail cherries and
2 long straws.

*Perfect as an aperitif, it can be
enjoyed throughout the day.*

PARADISE

Ingredients for 1 cocktail
gin 4,5 cl (1 1/2 oz)
Apricot Brandy
(apricot liqueur) 3 cl (1 oz)
orange juice 2 cl (2/3 oz)

% ALC/VOL: **18.3**
CALORIES: **188**

Origins and oddities
According to legend, this cocktail was
created around the 1920s, in honor of
Hawaii.

Preparation
Measure 4,5 cl (1 1/2 oz) of gin in a
graduated cylinder and pour into a shaker.
Repeat with 3 cl (1 oz) of Apricot Brandy and
2 cl (2/3 oz) of orange juice.
Add ice cubes and shake vigorously for a
few seconds. pour into a cup pre-chilled in
the freezer and serve, garnished with 1/2 an
orange slice.

*A fantastic drink, the Paradise can be
enjoyed at all hours of the day.*

PUCCINI

Ingredients for 1 cocktail
tangerine juice 3 cl (1 oz)
sparkling brut or champagne
9 cl (3 oz)

% ALC/VOL: **7.8** • CALORIES: **96**

Origins and oddities
According to legend, this cocktail was
created in 1948 by Renato Hausmann, a
bartender at the Hotel Posta in Cortina
d'Ampezzo, Italy.

Preparation
Measure 3 cl (1 oz) of tangerine juice in a
graduated cylinder and pour into a cup pre-
chilled in the freezer. Fill almost to the brim
with 9 cl (3 oz) of fresh sparkling brut or
champagne. Stir gently with a long-handled
spoon and serve.

*An elegant aperitif that can be served
throughout the day.*

ROSSINI

Ingredients for 1 cocktail
strawberries 3 cl (1 oz)
sparkling brut or champagne 9 cl (3 oz)
strawberry syrup (optional) 1 cl (1/4 oz)
natural water 3 cl (1 oz)

% ALC/VOL: **7.8** • CALORIES: **90**

Origins and oddities
A variation of the Bellini, the Rossini seems
tohave been invented in the mid-twentieth
century, in honor of the famous Italian
composer.

Preparation
Puree 5-6 medium-sized strawberries with
1 cl (1/4 oz) of strawberry syrup and
3 cl (1 oz) of natural water (measured
in a graduated cylinder).
Separate 3 cl (1 oz) of the
puree and pour it in a cup
pre-chilled in the freezer.
Add 9 cl (3 oz) of well-chilled
sparkling brut and stir gently
with a long-handle spoon. Serve,
garnished as desired with fresh
strawberries.

*To be enjoyed at any hour
of the day, the Rossini is
excellent as an aperitif.*

SALLY

Ingredients for 1 cocktail
dry vodka 3 cl (1 oz)
Aperol 3 cl (1 oz)
Campari 1 cl (1/4 oz)
Mandarinetto Isolabella
2 cl (2/3 oz)

% ALC/VOL: **18.8**
CALORIES: **112**

Origins and oddities
This new drink, created by Italian barman Giangranco Di Niso, came in first place in a national 2003 cocktail competition.

Preparation
Measure 3 cl (1 oz) of vodka in a graduated cylinder and pour into a low tumbler filled with ice. Repeat with 3 cl (1 oz) of Aperol, 2 cl (2/3 oz) of Mandarinetto Isolabella and 1 cl (1/4 oz) of Campari. Stir with a long-handled spoon and serve, garnished with 1/2 an orange slice and 2 cherries.

A delicious appetizer that will brighten your days.

SAMOA

Ingredients for 1 cocktail
dry vodka 5 cl (1 1/2 oz)
peach liqueur 2 cl (1/2 oz)
Campari 2 cl (1/2 oz)

% ALC/VOL: **22.9** • CALORIES: **150**

Origins and oddities
It seems that this drink was invented around the mid-'80s in a New York City bar when a couple wanted a new drink. The bartender named the resulting cocktail in honor of the island where the lovers had just spent a wonderful holiday.

Preparation
Measure 50 ml (3 1/3 tbsp) of vodka in a graduated cylinder and pour into a carafe. Repeat with 20 ml (4 tsp) of Campari and 20 ml (4 tsp) of peach liqueur. Add some ice cubes and stir with a long-handled spoon for several seconds. Pour into a cup (pre-chilled in the freezer), holding the ice back with the help of the spoon. To serve, garnish with 1/2 an orange slice and 1 cherry.

Excellent as an aperitif and during celebratory summer nights.

SPRITZ

Ingredients for 1 cocktail
Aperol 3 cl (1 oz)
dry sparkling wine 3 cl (1 oz)
soda water or sparkling water 3 cl (1 oz)

% ALC/VOL: **5.2** • CALORIES: **50**

Origins and oddities
The legend says that during their stay in Triveneto, Austrian soldiers found the local wines to be very strong. As a result, they started to sprinkle soda water in the wine to lower the alcohol content. The new mixture was therefore called Spritz, which in German means "spray".

Preparation
Measure 3 cl (1 oz) of Aperol in a graduated cylinder and pour into a low tumbler filled with ice. Repeat with 3 cl (1 oz) of dry sparkling wine and 3 cl (1 oz) of soda water (measured in a graduated cylinder). Stir gently for a few seconds and serve, garnished with 2 short straws and 1/2 an orange slice.

A light aperitif with low alcohol content, it is suitable for every hour of the day, but especially during Happy Hour.

STRAWBERRY CAIPIROSKA

Ingredients for 1 cocktail
dry vodka 6 cl (2 oz)
fresh strawberries 3-4
lime 1/2
white or cane sugar
about 20 g (about 1 1/2 tbsp)
strawberry or sugar syrup
1,5 cl (1/2 oz)

% ALC/VOL: **18.8** • CALORIES: **234**

Origins and oddities
The Caipiroska is a modern take on the
Caipirinha, Brazil's famous cocktail originally
made of cachaça (distilled sugar cane).

Preparation
Place 1/2 a lime, cut into cubes, in a low
tumbler. Add about 20 g (about 1 1/2 tbsp)
of sugar, 1,5 cl (1/2 oz) strawberry or sugar
syrup and 3-4 fresh strawberries. Grind
everything with a pestle until you have a
paste. Add crushed ice and 6 cl (2 oz)
of dry vodka (measured in a graduated
cylinder). Stir for a few seconds with a long
handled spoon, so that the Ingredients are
well blended. Serve, garnished with 2 short
straws and beautiful fresh strawberries.

*This drink is suitable for all times of the
day, and is well-loved by younger drinkers,
particularly those who make a habit of
Happy Hour.*

TESTAROSSA ICE

Ingredients for 1 cocktail
dry vodka 4,5 cl (1 1/2 oz)
Campari 4,5 cl (1 1/2 oz)
strawberry ice cream
about 100 g (about 4 oz)

% ALC/VOL: **25.6** • CALORIES: **275**

Origins and oddities
A drink created in 2007 by a bartender who
was particularly fond of Formula 1, in honor
of the last world championship won by the
Ferrari team.

Preparation
Measure 4,5 cl (1 1/2 oz) of vodka in a
graduated cylinder and pour into a blender.
Repeat with 4,5 cl (1 1/2 oz) of Campari.
Add about 100 g (about 4 oz) of strawberry
ice cream and 1/2 a low tumbler of crushed
ice. Blend for 15-20 seconds and pour
into a tall tumbler. Serve, garnished with 2
strawberries and 2 long straws.

An excellent aperitif.

VODKA MARTINI BOND

Ingredients for 1 cocktail
dry vodka 7,5 cl (2 1/2 oz)
dry vermouth 1,5 cl (1/2 oz)

% ALC/VOL: **25.8** • CALORIES: **198**

Origins and oddities
A successful remake of the classic Martini,
this drink was named after the famous agent
007, who in his films often orders a Vodka
Martini Cocktail.

Preparation
Measure 7,5 cl (2 1/2 oz) of vodka in a
graduated cylinder and pour into a shaker.
Repeat with 1,5 cl (1/2 oz) of dry
vermouth. Add a few ice cubes
and shake vigorously for a few
seconds. Pour into a cup pre-
chilled in the freezer and serve,
garnished with 2-3 previously
rinsed green olives, skewered on a
long toothpick, and a lemon rind.

*Very dry and very strong,
this remains one of the most popular
drinks in the world.*

ALPHABETICAL INDEX OF RECIPES

ALPHABETICAL INDEX OF COCKTAIL INGREDIENTS

ACADEMIA BARILLA.
AMBASSADOR OF ITALIAN CUISINE IN THE WORLD

In the heart of Parma, recognized as one of the most prestigious capitals of cuisine, the Barilla Center stands in the middle of Barilla's historical headquarters, now hosting Academia Barilla's modern structure. Founded in 2004 with the aim of affirming the role of Italian culinary arts, protecting the regional gastronomic heritage, defending it from imitations and counterfeits and to valorize the great tradition of Italian cooking, Academia Barilla is where great professionalism and unique competences in the world of cuisine meet. The institution organizes cooking courses for those passionate about food culture, offering services dedicated to the operators in the sector and proposing products of unparalleled quality. Academia Barilla was awarded the "Business-Culture Prize" for its promotional activities regarding gastronomic culture and Italian creativity in the world.

Our headquarters were designed to meet the educational needs in the field of food preparation and has the multimedia tools necessary to host large events: around an extraordinary gastronomic auditorium, there is an internal restaurant, a multisensory laboratory and various classrooms equipped with the most modern technology. In our Gastronomic Library we conserve over 11,000 volumes regarding specific topics and an unusual collection of historical menus and printed materials on the culinary arts: the library's enormous cultural heritage is available online and allows anyone to access hundreds of digitalized historical texts. This forward thinking organization and the presence of an internationally renowned team of professors guarantee a wide rage of courses, able to satisfy the needs of both catering professionals as well as simple cuisine enthusiasts. Academia Barilla also organizes cultural events and initiatives for highlighting culinary sciences open to the public, with the participation of experts, chefs and food critics. It also promotes the "Cinema Award", especially for short-length films dedicated to Italian food traditions.

www.academiabarilla.it

WS White Star Publishers® is a registered trademark
property of De Agostini Libri S.p.A.

© 2014 De Agostini Libri S.p.A.
Via G. da Verrazano, 15
28100 Novara, Italy
www.whitestar.it - www.deagostini.it

Translation and Editing: Arancho Doc

ISBN 978-88-544-0905-7
1 2 3 4 5 6   18 17 16 15 14

Printed in Italy